W9-APB-488

Royal Mother

Mount Mary College
LIBRARY
WITHDRAWN
56 - 1394

❧ Royal Mother ❧

The Story of
Queen Mother Elizabeth
and Her Family

by

Jennifer Ellis

Prentice-Hall, Inc.   New York

Copyright 1954 by

JENNIFER ELLIS

All rights reserved, including the right to reproduce
this book, or any portions thereof, in any form, except for the inclusion of brief quotations in a review.

Printed in the United States of America
By The Haddon Craftsmen, Scranton, Pa.
Library of Congress Catalog Card Number: 54-10509

First printing .... October, 1954
Second printing .... October, 1954

921
EL492E

Royal Mother

Chapter *1*

THIS is a story that might well begin "once upon a time" for it has all the elements of an old-time fairy tale. There is a King's son—the quiet unassuming younger son of storybook tradition—called by fate to step into his brother's place, to rule a great empire, and to be beloved as few sovereigns have been. There is a little girl, the daughter of a Scottish laird but with the blood of kings in her veins, growing up in a grim old castle to such grace and charm that she won all hearts, and among them that of the Prince. And finally there is the fairy-tale ending of a perfect marriage, and of a husband and wife who "lived happily ever after" until——

But let us leave that "until," for it is not yet, and instead look back to that year of grace 1905, when a ten-year-old boy and a five-year-old girl met at a children's party and the threads of two destinies were entwined.

The sun of Victorian splendor was already setting on the world into which those two children—Prince Albert, second son of the Duke of York, and the Lady Elizabeth

Bowes-Lyon, daughter of the fourteenth Earl of Strath-more—were born, but although storm clouds were beginning to gather on the far horizon, Britain's future seemed safe and untroubled. British diplomacy, backed by British sea power, was still strong enough to rule the nations; British goods, backed by British capital, were supreme in every market. Industry was booming; income tax was low. The great landowners could afford to keep up any number of town and country houses, staffed by large and contented households. Life moved at the leisurely pace of the landau and the governess' cart rather than the motor, which was still an object of distrust. There was time for gracious entertaining, beautiful manners, the arts of letter-writing and conversation. It was an era of security, good living—relatively for all classes—comfortable thinking, and big and united families.

The little Lady Elizabeth Bowes-Lyon, who was born on the fourth of August, 1900, was the youngest but one of ten children. It was a conveniently spaced family, broken into groups. Between Lady Mary, the eldest surviving daughter, and Lord Glamis, the eldest son, there was only a year, and from their nursery days they paired off together. Then, after an interval, came in quick succession three boys, who formed a unit of their own. Then another pair, a girl—Lady Rose—and a boy—Michael—and finally, many years later, Lady Elizabeth and her brother David, who arrived just fifteen months after her. Between these youngest and the rest of the family there was so wide a gap that their mother used to call them "The Two Benjamins," and say that people would take them for her grandchildren. They were as inseparable as twins, playing in a world of their own, against a background of big brothers who brought home their cricketing friends in the summer holidays, and big sisters just on the point of leaving the schoolroom and putting up their hair.

She was a lovely child, this youngest daughter of the Bowes-Lyons, who could trace their ancestry back in an unbroken line over six centuries; far further than most of the reigning houses of Europe. She had inherited their combination of dark brown hair and vivid—almost sapphire —blue eyes; a type of beauty so often associated with Ireland but found in most Celtic races. The contrast was heightened in her by the wild-rose skin of her mother's family, the Cavendish-Bentincks, which has produced some of the most beautiful women in English history.

In spite of her apparent fragility—she was tiny as a child, with an elfin grace in all her movements, and exquisitely made hands and feet—she was a tomboy, taught to romp and play games by schoolboy brothers. Almost as soon as she was out of a high chair she was riding her little Shetland pony "Bobs," and there was not a tree in the gardens of St. Paul's Waldenbury which she could not climb. She had even in those days the fearlessness and love of adventure which has prompted her now, in the fifties, to interest herself in flying.

On her father's side she had the heritage of a fighting race. It was no tame and conventional strain which she would pass on to the future sovereigns of England. To the earlier generations of Lyons, warfare was incidental to survival. Through turbulent centuries they held their own in fierce feuds and border raids—where victory went to the strongest and quarter was neither asked nor given.

Glamis Castle, Lord Strathmore's Scottish seat in Forfarshire, where the family spent three months every autumn, still bears witness to this stormy past. Rising from the hollow of a grassy plain and protected by the Grampian and Sidlaw Hills, it was planned by its eleventh-century architect to be fortress as well as home. Its massive stone towers and walls, fifteen feet thick in places, have defied generations of foes. It came into the possession of the Strathmore family nearly six hundred years ago, as part of the dowry of Princess Jean, daughter of King Robert II of Scotland, who married her father's Keeper of the Privy Seal, Sir John Lyon.

Although its romantic link with Macbeth is believed to be only legendary, the very stones of Glamis are steeped in tradition. Nearly every room has its history. The great spiral staircase, up which the Bowes-Lyon children—and later the Princesses Elizabeth and Margaret—loved to race, once echoed to the tread of the knights carrying the wounded King Malcolm II upstairs to the bedroom in which he died. It still bears his name, and the stains said to have been made by his blood could be seen on the floor until it was boarded over quite recently.

In another room Mary Queen of Scots slept on her way north to quell Lord Huntley's rebellion. The menu of the dinner ordered for her and her Four Maries is still in existence. Then there is "Sir Walter Scott's Room," draped with the Bard's own tartan, and another bedroom which is never used, no matter how many guests may be staying at the castle, for its name—"The Hangman's Chamber"—is a grim reminder of the fact that the last two occupants were both found hanged there.

The room most sacred to memory is "Prince Charlie's" where the last of the Stuarts slept during his wanderings, and had to flee so hurriedly from his pursuers the next morning that he left his watch under his pillow. It is still—with a sword and a suit of clothes once worn by him—among the family's most cherished possessions.

There are many Stuart relics at Glamis, for the Lyons of the past were staunch followers of "The King Over the Water." Each succeeding generation was imbued with sentimental attachment to the lost cause, and the little Lady Elizabeth—who would one day marry a descendant of the House of Hanover—learned almost from her cradle the haunting old Jacobite songs and legends of her ancestors.

Probably no house in Britain has had so many stories of the supernatural attached to it as Glamis. Even the members of the Bowes-Lyon family do not know the precise origin and history of all the ghosts who are said to haunt the older parts of the Castle, but the children to whom the great gloomy staircase, vaulted crypt and long eerie passages, lit only by lamps or candles, represented home, were untroubled by its sinister reputation.

"There was nothing in the least menacing in the atmosphere," Lady Rose Bowes-Lyon (now Lady Granville), the Queen Mother's elder sister, told me. "You always felt that if there were any ghosts at Glamis they were friendly ones. Personally I never had any evidence of them, but my brother David as a child used to tell us that he saw shadowy people—'gray people,' he called them—in some of the rooms and passages. And I remember Elizabeth saying once or twice that she had met a strange lady on the staircase, who had smiled at her and passed by without speaking. The dress she described seemed to belong to the sixteenth century, but we never identified the lady."

One of Lady Rose's recollections of her youngest sister as a child is very typical of the Queen Mother.

It was a wild autumn evening, with the wind rising to a shriek round the Castle. Lady Strathmore had gone up to her room to dress for dinner when Elizabeth and David came to say good night to their mother before going to bed. Suddenly the eight-year-old David remembered that he had left his story book in the crypt, where they had been playing that afternoon.

By that time he was becoming aware of the current gossip about the Glamis ghosts, and did not care for the idea of going into the dim crypt alone. He asked his mother to let him ring for one of the footmen to accompany him.

"Certainly not," said Lady Strathmore firmly. "There is nothing to be afraid of. You don't need anyone to take you. You must go by yourself."

David's face blanched, but he squared his shoulders manfully and left the room. A little figure slipped out very quietly immediately after him and Elizabeth's hand was put into his. "David," she said, with a faint tremor in her voice, "Mother said you were not to ring for someone to go with you, but she didn't say you couldn't have me."

Hand in hand the brother and sister set off to brave King Malcolm's ghost, or whatever unknown horror lurked on the staircase.

The protective instinct was always very strong in Elizabeth. Her sister remembers the funny little maternal way she had with her brother, although he was only fifteen months younger. Seing him once at a children's party—when she herself was about six—brushing cake crumbs off the corner of his mouth with one hand, she cast an anxious glance at the hostess and hurriedly passed him her own handkerchief.

"David's very young still," she said in tender excuse for him.

To the two youngest Bowes-Lyon children Glamis offered endless possibilities of entertainment. On sunny days there were the gardens to play in, with the woods beyond, and farther still the moors, where the older members of the family and relays of guests went shooting, to return in the late afternoon with bulging bags of grouse and woodcock.

Elizabeth and David regarded the woods as their own special territory, a natural setting for their favorite game of Red Indians. People on the estate still remember the two little figures racing through the russet autumn leaves, their homemade bows and arrows slung round their necks, their faces daubed with paint and crowned with feathers.

On more sedate occasions they were accompanied either by Lord Strathmore or by William Fairweather, the head keeper of the Glamis estate, and sworn friend and ally of their childhood, who taught them to shoot and fish in the river Dean, build rafts and make a camp fire. Elizabeth loved best of all to go out with her father, who was a mine of information where his beloved woods were concerned. Like many countrymen, he had the soul of a poet and a deep feeling for nature. Every tree was his friend; every bird's call had its own significance for him. He passed on much of his knowledge to his youngest daughter. Years

afterward she instilled into her own children the same love
of nature, and spent many happy hours rambling with
them over the moors round Birkhall, teaching them the
simple botany and country lore which she had learned from
her father and William Fairweather.

On wet days Glamis was paradise to an adventurous
child. Its honeycomb of passages, mural chambers built
into the solid bulk of the walls, and secret staircases leading to the roof, lent themselves to endless games of hide-
and-seek and sardines. The great stone crypt was a perfect
background for charades. Then there was the stillroom,
with its inviting warmth and homely odors of spices and
hot bread, to be raided for crystallized cherries and biscuits
straight from the oven. Elizabeth was always fascinated by
this room, where two stillroom maids worked all day, under
the supervision of the housekeeper, making the buns,
scones, cakes and jams for the big Scottish teas which
were a tradition at Glamis. Sometimes—if you were tactful
and chose a favorable moment—you would be allowed to
shape your own little bun out of the mass of dough, or even
to roll out a gingerbread pig, with currants for eyes, and
that was a treat indeed.

Best of all joys were the two big dressing-up chests
kept in the crypt, filled with all sorts of costumes—brocaded
dresses, cloaks, hats, wigs, masks, fans, lengths of silk and
velvet—in fact everything a child could need for the game
of make-believe. They were a source of unfailing inspiration
to both Elizabeth and her brother.

If Glamis stood for the stormy past and rugged splendor of Scotland, St. Paul's Waldenbury, Lord Strathmore's
Hertfordshire seat where the family spent the greater part

of every year, seemed to hold the very spirit of the English countryside. It was a mellow, peaceful old Adam house, framed in gardens with long shady alleys, moss-grown statues and fountains, and hedges of yew and hawthorn clipped into the forms of birds and animals. The Queen Mother's earliest, and perhaps happiest, childhood memories are of this sun-wrapped Hertfordshire home—of the drone of bees among the flower beds; the cooing of the wood-pigeons; the scents of honeysuckle and new-mown hay; of the dairy where she used to run in hot from play for a glass of cool foaming milk. Most of all of her nursery, with its high old-fashioned fireguard, its story pictures, framed by the gardener, and its big rocking-horse. This horse—rather worn by the time she inherited him, as the ninth child of the family—was her first love. She could imagine nothing more beautiful than his flowing mane— thinned out a little by clutching fingers—flaming nostrils, and proudly poised head, with the paint rubbed thin at one place from her fervent kisses. Mounted on his back she would rock ecstatically to an unknown destination, just as her daughter Princess Elizabeth would do twenty-five years later in that same nursery, and on that well-worn and beloved rocking-horse.

At the bottom of the garden at St. Paul's Waldenbury —and also dear to memory—was the wood; carpeted with primroses and anemones in spring, and peopled . . . she was sure of it in those childhood days . . . by fairies. She used to look for them, in between the trees, when she and David picnicked there. She could have sworn she heard them whispering in the leaves. Yet none of them told her that it would be a place of destiny for her, or that on a

January morning many years later she would make a decision there that would ultimately lead her to share a Throne.

While the two youngest Bowes-Lyon children were
romping in the hayfield at St. Paul's Waldenbury, or chas-
ing one another down the passages at Glamis, a little boy
was playing at York Cottage, Sandringham, organized
games under the watchful eye of his tutor; or drilling with
his elder brother and sister at the command of a Sergeant-
Major. Prince Albert, second son of the then Prince of
Wales, had only a five years' start in life ahead of the Lady
Elizabeth Bowes-Lyon, but they were years weighted with
the responsibilities of Royal birth. While she was getting
up when the dew was still on the grass, for the sheer joy of
being out in the sunshine of a summer morning, and running down the garden to give her chickens an early feeding,
he was beginning the day's lessons with half an hour's
preparation at his desk before breakfast. Discipline already
figured prominently in his life. The simple nursery and
schoolroom quarters at Sandringham were ruled by a clockwork routine. The Prince of Wales (who would later be
King George V) was stern with himself and with his sons.
He gave them justice and kindness but without what he
would have called "sentimentality." His second son—
"Bertie," as he was always known in the family—was destined for the Navy. His father, who had served in it and
delighted in the life, was determined to make a sailor of
him. In his view the fact that the boy was sensitive, shy,
and handicapped by a persistent stammer, was all the more
reason for toughening him.

The Princess of Wales—later Queen Mary—was more

indulgent with her children, and saw to it that in their planned lives some space was left for the normal amusements of childhood. She arranged dancing classes for them and allowed them to attend children's parties in their own circle during the winter months when they were at Marlborough House with their parents. The sociable elder brother, Prince Edward (later the Duke of Windsor) was in his element at parties and usually led all the games, but for many years they were an ordeal to the shy Bertie, who hated dressing in a stiff Eton suit and dancing with a succession of sedate, elaborately sashed and hair-ribboned little girls. But one day there came the party that was different.

It was given at Montagu House by the Duchess of Buccleuch for her grandchildren. It was the usual Edwardian children's party, with a magician and a magic lantern, but perhaps because the hostess was one of the greatest in an era famed for great hostesses, and so fond of children that she delighted in bringing all her talents to bear on entertaining them—or perhaps for some other cause—that party seems to have lived in the memories of all the children who were there. I have talked to several of them and they still have a smile of recollection for that best-party-ever of more than forty-five years ago. And strangely not one of them has forgotten a little girl of five years old, with long dark hair escaping from the conventional bow of ribbon, and blue eyes shining like sapphires with the joy of her first London party.

The guest who remembered her best of all was the little boy who sat next to her at tea, a shy little boy in an Eton suit, whose rather lonely heart was warmed and comforted because she neither showed impatience at his stam-

Mount Mary College
LIBRARY
56-1394

Chapter 2

In that prosperous, unclouded first decade of the new century there were already signs of a changing world. The Conservative Party, split within itself over the question of free trade, was defeated in the general elections of 1906. The Liberals romped into power, and with them a fiery young Welshman, David Lloyd George. There was talk of increased taxation; of cutting down the privileges of the landowners.

To the little Lady Elizabeth, secure in the setting of a large and very happy household, these distant portents meant nothing. Lord Strathmore—although the family was by no means rich in terms of money today—employed almost a small army of men and women. The indoor staff at Glamis Castle alone numbered between twenty-five and thirty; the estate, with its gardens, home farm, woods and shoot, accounted for many more. In addition there were the two other country seats—St. Paul's Waldenbury, and Streatlam Castle in County Durham—and the London house in St. James's Square. The whole formed a com-

19

munity, run on almost feudal lines, democratic after the fashion of the old Scottish clans. Lady Strathmore knew not only the names of all those who served her but every detail of their lives. She took the same personal interest in them as in her own sons and daughters. If a gardener's boy proved to have a flair for growing flowers, he was promoted. If a scullery maid showed promise as a cook, she was taken away from her sink and given special training. Nothing ever escaped the observation of the mistress of the household, for—in much the same way as the chatelaines of the Middle Ages—she was the center of all its activities. Although she had a housekeeper she was familiar with the running of every department, for she had been trained in her girlhood to the Victorian standard of competence in all the housewifely arts. She knew more about the growing of flowers than her own gardeners, more about jam-making than her housekeeper, and could repair a torn tablecloth more neatly than any of her housemaids.

The stillroom especially was her province. She had any number of old family recipes for every kind of preserve, homemade wine and liqueur; simple beauty preparations—lotions for whitening the hands and clearing the skin—and homely country remedies. She passed them on to her daughters and to this day, when she has a cold or a sore throat, the Queen Mother flies to the old-fashioned linseed tea and hot lemon-and-honey drinks of Glamis.

Her childhood was spent in an atmosphere of love and security which played an important part in moulding not only her own character but those of her daughters. Its influence extends today into the lives of Prince Charles and Princess Anne, for their mother comes of a line of women with whom homemaking was a tradition. Lady Strathmore had—as one of the Queen Mother's closest friends told me —a genius for motherhood. It was inherited by all her daughters and in full measure by the youngest, Lady Elizabeth. As the baby of the family she was closer to her mother than the rest, and grew up resembling her in many ways. Both had the same tact and graciousness of manner, and their voices were so alike that even members of the family were often deceived. That clear, exceptionally beautiful speaking voice which is one of the Queen Mother's greatest charms is a heritage passed from mother to daughter for several generations. Both The Queen and Princess Margaret have inherited it.

Lady Strathmore was one of those rare people who excel at everything they take up. Without being in any way erudite—she had the Victorian horror of a "Blue Stocking"—she was very well educated, spoke several languages, and had read widely. It had been the fashion when she was a girl to dabble in the arts; instead she had studied them seriously. She was a talented painter and a brilliant pianist. All her children had their first music lessons from her, and Elizabeth was firmly grounded in the classics. She played Bach and Beethoven when she was eight, but she loved best of all the beautiful old Scottish songs which she picked up—no one knew exactly how or from whom for she was heard playing them when she was supposed to be practicing her very first exercises. She has the gift, now shared by Princess Margaret, of being able to play anything from ear. Both of them can come home from a dance or a show and reproduce perfectly any tune they have heard there.

Another talent of Lady Strathmore's was for needle-
work. She embroidered exquisitely, never using a pattern
even for the most intricate designs. Many examples of her
work are still at Glamis. One of the most beautiful is an
exact copy of a Jacobean bedstead. The original, which had
been in the family for over two hundred years, was faded
and worm-eaten beyond recognition, but Lady Strathmore
set to work, with multi-colored silks on a satin background,
and made a perfect reproduction. Under the valance she
embroidered—as an individual touch—the names of all her
sons and daughters.

The Edwardians believed that children should be seen
and not heard, banished to the nursery or schoolroom, and
brought up by nurses and governesses. Lady Strathmore
had other views. She herself gave all her children their first
lessons. Elizabeth learned to count, to tell the time, and to
spell words of one syllable on mother's knee—as her own
daughters would do later. At six she could read most of her
story books from cover to cover and repeat a number of
psalms. She learned exceptionally quickly, leaving her
brother David, to his chagrin, far behind.

Instead of being kept out of sight, like most of their
contemporaries, the Bowes-Lyon children had the run of
the house, came down to meals with their parents in the
big dining room as soon as they were old enough to sit at
the table, and were encouraged to talk to guests. Consequently, they grew up without a trace of self-consciousness.
Elizabeth, especially, had all the social graces almost from
her babyhood. Lady Strathmore was insistent on the question of manners, and she herself taught her daughters what
had been called in her own girlhood "deportment." They

learned how to enter and leave a room; how to sit down and get up again gracefully; how to accept a present and thank the giver appreciatively. All this without realizing that they were learning, for their mother was clever enough to present the lesson in the form of a charade, in which some of the family had to do the acting while others guessed what they were representing. They saw it as fun, but it was splendid training—most of all for the daughter who would one day have to do all these simple things with the eyes of thousands upon her. She followed the same plan with her own children with the result that all through their childhood neither of the Princesses ever showed any awkwardness or shyness in public.

In the nursery, too, good manners were exacted by Alah—or to give her her full name, Clara Cooper Knight, the devoted nurse who served two generations with such fidelity. Alah, as she was always called, came to St. Paul's Waldenbury as a young woman of twenty-four, to take charge of the month-old Lady Elizabeth Bowes-Lyon. Alah remained with her until after her eleventh birthday, and then left, with many tears, to go to her eldest sister, Lady Elphinstone, who had by that time a young family. But Alah had not said goodbye either to the most dearly loved of all her babies or to the homely old nursery at St. Paul's Waldenbury, for many years after she returned to the young Duchess of York to nurse her daughters, the Princesses Elizabeth and Margaret, and she remained with them until her death.

Alah had the most loyal heart in the world. But she never allowed love to blind her to the failings of any of the children of whom she had charge. The high standard

which she set for them made her severe. She insisted on
punctuality and tidiness—two virtues which had top priority
in her well-ordered and disciplined mind. Toys had to be
put away carefully. An old and battered one must never
be thrown aside because its small owner had tired of it.

"It gave you pleasure once," she would say in her stern
way. "You must remember that and be grateful." A rather
charming lesson for life.

Another—and still remaining—link with those early
days is Mme. Guèrin, formerly Mlle. Lang, who went as
French governess to the Bowes-Lyon children when Lady
Elizabeth was only four-and-a-half years old. It is an association that has never lapsed for although "Madé,"—as they
called her in abbreviation of Mademoiselle—left at the end
of seven years to be married, her daughter came over to
England in her turn to teach French to the Princesses
Elizabeth and Margaret.

Mme. Guèrin has a vivid recollection of the little
Elizabeth Bowes-Lyon, who danced into the hall at St.
Paul's Waldenbury and held out her hand to the newly
arrived French governess. "I do hope you'll be happy here,"
she said in her quaint grown-up fashion.

"She was an enchanting child," Mme. Guèrin told me.
"Lovely to look at, with her tiny hands and feet and rose-leaf
coloring—like a Dresden china figure, perfect in miniature.
But what was so charming about her was her friendliness and
complete lack of self-consciousness. It was so amusing to find
a child of her age with the tact and *savoir faire* of a grown-up
person. I remember that when I had been with the family
only a few months some visitors arrived unexpectedly to call
on Lady Strathmore, who happened to be out. On going

downstairs a little later to look for Elizabeth I found her in the drawing room, calmly dispensing tea for them, pouring out and making conversation exactly as she had seen her mother do."

"You see, Madé," she explained afterward, "I thought they would be tired after their drive, and it would be so disappointing for them to have to go away again without seeing Mother, so I just rang for tea and asked them to stay—and they did."

But although she was a gracious child, with the tact springing from kindness and a sensitive nature, she was a thoroughly human and very merry little girl, brimming over with high spirits and delighting to play practical jokes. One was to lie in wait with David on the roof of Glamis Castle for the arrival of visitors and then deluge them with water from a garden hose—a form of entertainment which came to a speedy end when it was discovered by Lady Strathmore.

Another of Mme. Guèrin's memories is of Elizabeth coming in from a garden party which was being held at Glamis in aid of some charity. One of the attractions had been a palmist. "Did you have your hand read?" asked Madé. Elizabeth, who was then about seven, laughed.

"Yes, I did. But she was silly. She says I'm going to be a Queen when I grow up."

"That you can't be, unless they change the laws of England for you," said the practical Mademoiselle.

Elizabeth tossed her hat on a chair. "Who wants to be a Queen anyway?" Dancing round the room she began to sing the old French nursery rhyme which she had just learned, *S'il fleurisse je serai reine.*

She was a born dancer, light as thistledown on her feet,

and could pick up any steps without effort—a gift which has been inherited by her daughter Princess Margaret. Lady Strathmore, who had loved dancing in her girlhood, taught both Elizabeth and David simple steps almost as soon as they could walk, and then handed them over to Mr. Neal, a Scottish dancing master of the old school. From him they learned the reels, the polka and the waltz, and some of the old-time dances in which he specialized. For these they very often put on fancy dresses, taken from the dressing-up chest.

"I shall always remember them dancing the minuet together at Glamis," Mme. Guèrin told me. "In the somber dining room of the Castle with its panelled walls they made a lovely picture. The two children, David, very fair, wearing a jester's costume with cap and bells, and Elizabeth, with her dark hair hanging on her shoulders, pointing her toes daintily under the long red silk seventeenth-century dress which her mother had made for her, while the old dancing master circled round them, his violin tucked up against his venerable white beard, his keen eyes following every step."

When the dancing lesson was over Elizabeth would curtsy and David would achieve a courtly bow. Then they would tear off their fancy dresses and race out into the garden.

No child could have had a happier or freer life than this one who was destined to share a Throne. All through the long spring and summer months when the family were at St. Paul's Waldenbury she played with her brother in the garden, helped the farm workers to get in the hay, and shared their tea in a shady corner of the field afterwards. She picnicked in "The Fairies' Wood," with the tomato sandwiches and homemade cakes spread out under the big

oak which housed her own specially beloved ring-doves.
She had a passion for pets and kept an assortment—rabbits,
frogs, turtles, kittens of all colors and ages, a goat, even a
baby pig, which grew so intelligent that there were heart-
broken tears when it was pronounced too old for its sheltered existence and had to be sold. There were newts and
caterpillars—to the horror of Alah, who never knew where
she would come upon them—and innumerable birds, in addition to Bobby the privileged bullfinch. Many of them had
been rescued with injured wings or other disabilities and
tenderly nursed back to health. When one of them died it
was laid in a wooden pencil box lined with rose leaves and
given an impressive funeral, with David in the role of sex-
ton and Elizabeth preaching a long sermon, punctuated by
tears.

The best loved of all her pets was her tiny Shetland
pony, Bobs, which used to follow her in and out of the
house, and even up and down the stairs. There were dogs
too of various breeds and a whole colony of cats.

The cat population at St. Paul's Waldenbury was
mainly concentrated in and around a dilapidated old brew
house in the grounds, aptly named "The Flea House." It
had long been in disuse and, as the only approach to it was
a rotten wooden staircase, not strong enough to bear the
weight of an adult, it was more or less abandoned to the
generations of kittens who had first seen the light of day in
the old bins and chests which had never been taken away.
It was the favorite sanctuary of the two youngest Bowes-
Lyons, particularly when conscience suggested the advis-
ability of a short absence. Its inaccessibility gave the illusion
of a citadel. To add to it they laid in a secret store of iron

rations—apples, oranges, candy and biscuits from the village shop; raisins and slabs of cooking chocolate coaxed out of the housekeeper; matches, candles, and a few packages of Woodbines which David was always going to smoke one day. Both of them still remember the thrill of running up the rickety stairs, deaf to the distant voices of authority calling to them from the garden, and eating a meal of sticky candy and stale biscuits.

Their amusements were simple compared to those of the children of today. The movies were still struggling against prejudice, and most parents frowned on the idea of taking small children to a performance. The circus, in its present sophisticated form, was almost unknown, though the traveling menagerie—"The Wild Beast Show" as it was called—visited most small towns. They were once taken to one and Elizabeth cried over the pathos of the aging lion pacing his cramped cage and the thin little monkeys shivering in the autumn wind. They never went again.

Parties too were few and far between, for social contacts—at least for children—in those days before motoring came into its own, were limited to families within radius of a carriage drive. But Elizabeth and David created their own fun for they had one priceless asset all too rare in the nursery world of today: scope for make-believe. The annual visit to the pantomime at Drury Lane was a thrill in itself, anticipated for weeks in advance, but it was also the inspiration for games for the rest of the year. Every item of the program was acted over and over again, with the aid of the dressing-up chest and a few homemade props. Elizabeth especially loved acting, and as she grew older showed a great deal of talent in amateur theatricals.

"She is a born comedienne," one of her oldest friends told me. "Whenever she took part in charades—which were very popular at house parties in those days, she used to have everyone convulsed with laughter. She would have made a wonderful music-hall artist, and so would Princess Margaret. Both of them have the same gift for mimicry and for holding an audience."

But in their early childhood visits to theatres were strictly limited for the two youngest Bowes-Lyons, for neither Lady Strathmore nor Alah believed in spoiling children. The Queen Mother can remember even now practically every pantomime she saw as a child, and that *Peter Pan* seemed almost the event of a lifetime.

Her father's London house stood for excitement to her, for Christmas parties and pantomimes, but it was never a home enshrined in memory like St. Paul's Waldenbury or Glamis.

Best of all she loved those autumn weeks at Glamis, with the moors purple with heather and the clear burns shining like amber; the sunsets splashed across the sky in crimson and gold; the sharp night air that made the crackling log fires in the enormous hearths at the Castle a welcome sight. She will always remember those days before the First World War; the contentment of a big family circle unbroken then—the friends who came up year after year for shooting and for the Cricket Week in August; the dinners by candlelight in the vast oak-panelled dining room, with the two pipers in their swinging kilts marching round the table. And sometimes, as a great treat, she was allowed to come down for dessert, demure in her long white frock and sash. She would sit up very straight on her high-backed

Chapter 3

In those same years at the close of King Edward VII's reign a boy at Osborne was winning his first battles. The Prince of Wales had sent his second son to the Naval Training College with the order to his tutor: "Treat him as a cadet and make him realize his responsibilities." The first part of the injunction was after Prince Albert's own heart; the second was unnecessary. Serious, inclined to be silent but deeply observant, he was already showing signs of a latent force of character and of a courage and determination far beyond his years. He had passed the entrance examination for Osborne with flying colors, not because he was a particularly brilliant scholar but through sheer perseverance. It was only the beginning of a valiant fight. All through those early years of his career, the training at Osborne and Dartmouth, and service with the Fleet later, he would be handicapped by almost continuous ill health. But he would not give in.

By the time the fifteen-year-old Prince Albert was preparing to go from Osborne to the Naval College at Dart-

mouth, Lady Elizabeth Bowes-Lyon was also beginning to
take life more seriously. By now she had progressed from
the nursery to the schoolroom, and although Lady Strathmore—unlike many mothers in that era of fashionable
boarding schools—insisted on keeping her daughter at
home, she had progressive ideas on education and engaged
highly qualified governesses for her. Elizabeth was given a
thorough grounding in all the usual subjects, and especially
in languages. Before she was fourteen she spoke fluent
French and German, and had picked up a useful smattering
of Italian—merely from occasional visits to Lady Strathmore's mother who had a villa in Florence. She has always
had an exceptionally quick ear for languages. A member of
her suite who accompanied her on her first visit to Kenya,
as Duchess of York, told me that in less than a fortnight
she could give orders in Swahili to the native boys.

In 1911 the beloved Madé left the Bowes-Lyon family
to become Mme. Guèrin and live in France. She still remembers first the dismay with which the news of the ap-
proaching parting was received by Elizabeth and David, and
then the whispered consultations over the form of her wedding present.

One day Elizabeth came to her and flung her arms
round her neck.

"I'm giving you a present with Mother and another
one with David, Madé darling," she said. "But I must give
you one which is really and truly mine." She heaved a sigh.
"I do wish I hadn't taken so much out of my money-box
at Christmas. I thought that perhaps Father might advance
me some money but he won't."

Lord Strathmore was strict in the matter of pocket

money. None of his children had more than ninepence a week until they were in their teens and if they overspent it, they were not allowed to borrow. In the end the housekeeper came to the rescue over the wedding present by devising small jobs—hulling strawberries and shelling peas were among them—for which payment could be honorably received. They brought in enough to buy a teaspoon for infusing tea, "because you like tea and you once said they didn't make as good tea in France as in England," the giver explained with pride.

Eventually David was allowed to share in the presentation, his money-box having yielded only tenpence-halfpenny and no more jobs being available. So an impressive card, which had taken brother and sister the whole afternoon to achieve, was attached to the parcel. Mme. Guèrin still has it in her possession: It reads:

TO MADÉ
WITH VERY BEST WISHES ON HER MARRIAGE
FROM
ELIZABETH AND DAVID

A postscript added the anxious afterthought:
"P.S.
      We Hope Edmont Will Be Kind To You."

The years slipped away; the last tranquil carefree years of a world that was passing for ever. To Elizabeth they brought few changes. Her eldest brother, Lord Glamis, married the daughter of the Duke of Leeds, and her eldest sister, Lady Mary, married Lord Elphinstone. She was bridesmaid at both weddings, and in due course became an aunt. She was separated from her adored brother David for the first time when he went away to school, and for a while was so lost without him that she flung herself into her lessons and passed her Junior Oxford exam. She began to study music seriously and took lessons—except when she was in Scotland—with Mme. Matilde Verne.

At Glamis Lady Strathmore supervised her piano practice and taught her to play the miniature organ in the chapel at the Castle. She herself played this instrument beautifully and always acted as organist at the Sunday services. When her daughter grew older she sometimes deputized for her. The family still smile over the recollection of the Sunday when the fifteen-year-old Elizabeth was suddenly inspired to brighten the service with a new voluntary. Instead of the strains of Handel, which they had been expecting, they heard variations on the theme of "Yip I Addy I Ay."

That drew forth a reprimand even from her father, who was devoted to her. The excuse that she could not think of anything else to play at the moment was not considered adequate!

Religious training played an important part in her background. Its influence is still a vital force both in her own life and in the lives of her daughters. Lord and Lady Strathmore had the ideals of the Victorian age in which they were born. They brought up their family in a strict moral code. Every day began with prayer, and there could be no shirking of church on Sunday, unless for illness or some exceptional reason. All the children learned Bible stories and psalms in the Scottish metrical version.

The summer of 1914 began like any other. Lessons with her governess in the morning; preparation or piano practice after tea; long lazy afternoons in the "enchanted wood" at St. Paul's Waldenbury, with a book and a basket of strawberries picked in the kitchen garden, and still hot from the sun. She was looking forward to her fourteenth birthday on the 4th of August. Already she had chosen her birthday treat—a visit to the theatre. She was having a new dress made for it; a longer one than any she had had yet. And after that there would be Glamis, with David home from Eton for the holidays, and her elder brothers and a big house party of their friends up for the shooting. There would be long days out with the guns on the moors; cold lunches from packed hampers, and real Scottish teas afterwards for ravenous appetites. And in the evening there would be a sing-song, with her sister Rose at the piano and everyone grouped round her, in the soft lamplight of the drawing room, singing "Over the Sea to Skye" and all the old songs she loved. Life was good at nearly fourteen!

In that summer a young midshipman was serving in H.M.S. *Collingwood,* which was then cruising in the Mediterranean; an unassuming young man, known simply in the gun-room as Prince Albert. To his superiors he was a hard-working conscientious officer who got up at six every morning, helped to coal ship when it was necessary and generally pulled his weight. To his mess he was someone who expected to be treated like everybody else, hated obsequiousness, and avoided anyone who reminded him of his Royal rank. Although he was shy he made friends easily, probably because he preferred listening to talking. He rarely spoke of his own affairs, and never about his health. Only the ship's surgeon knew that he suffered almost continuously from gastric trouble, and realized the extent of his courage.

Someone else realized it too—his father. And King George V had already said, "I am pleased with my son."

The 4th of August—that long-anticipated birthday—dawned and Elizabeth, glowing in her new dress, went to the theatre with her mother and brothers. But it was to look down from their box on a crowd cheering frenziedly, waving flags, singing patriotic songs—a crowd in the grip of war fever.

Young as she was, she was still old enough to bear the imprint of the war—like most of her generation. In less than a month the whole tempo of her life had changed. She went up to Glamis that autumn, but there was no shooting over the moors and no house party, for her elder brothers had all joined the Army, and the Castle had already been converted into a Red Cross hospital for convalescents. One of her most vivid memories is of that first war Christmas of 1914, with a giant Christmas tree set up in the crypt and a circle of men in hospital blue singing carols round it.

Looking back over the years she can still spotlight those wartime experiences. The unreality of the first months, with her established schoolroom routine upset and lesson books put aside while she went down to help her sister Rose and the nurses in the hospital. The thrill of being treated like a grown-up, and allowed to cope with all sorts of responsibilities—the catering, ordering of stores and bookkeeping, even though she could not do the actual nursing. The long winter evenings playing whist with the soldiers in the big ward, or leading them in sing-songs round the piano. And then, in 1915, the first sorrow of her young life—when her brother Fergus was killed at Loos.

There were still occasional visits to London too, although most of the house in St. James's Square was shut up and the staff had been reduced to the minimum. She loved to arrive there a week or two before the end of David's school term so that she could go down to Eton and have tea with him in his study—very much the elder sister sitting behind the tea pot and cutting him big slices of his favorite cherry cake, which she always took down with her.

With the rest of the family all engaged in war work, David and she were more or less left to their own devices when he came up to London for his school holidays. They spent most of their evenings going to theatres. As their pocket money was still strictly limited and they wanted to see as many plays as possible, they usually sat in the cheap seats. When the show was a popular one and their resources were scanty, they often had to stand in line for an hour or two, armed with bars of chocolate (a penny each in those days). Neither of them minded the long wait. They loved the theatre crowds, and the street singers and acrobats who entertained them.

Once, when funds were very low, Elizabeth decided on an appeal to her father. Going to the nearest station she wired him:

Strathmore, Glamis, Scotland
SOS; L.S.D.; R.S.V.P.
Elizabeth.

It was successful!

She grew up quickly, like so many children in those years. The war—and especially her responsibilities in the hospital at Glamis—had made her thoughtful for her age, and developed in her self-reliance and a capacity for quick thinking. People on the Glamis estate still remember her courage and initiative as a sixteen-year-old girl when a serious fire broke out at the Castle one night, and how she organized and directed a band of helpers who succeeded in salvaging all the pictures and valuables before the arrival of the Fire Brigade from Dundee. She has always been noted in her family for her cool head in an emergency, and her instant grasp of any situation. Even as a girl she was intensely practical. Her vivid interest in those around her made life an adventure.

To Prince Albert also the war brought new experiences. At the outbreak when his ship put out with the rest of the Fleet to Scapa Flow he was suffering from serious gastric trouble, but he refused even to consider a transfer to a post ashore. Within the first few weeks he became so much worse that he had to be put on board the hospital ship at Scapa and taken to the hospital at Aberdeen, where he was operated on for acute appendicitis. But no sooner was the operation over than he was back at his post.

Like every other man in the Fleet he shared the boredom of the long vigil at Scapa Flow and the relief at the news—on May 30, 1916—that the German Fleet was at last putting out to sea. The next evening, from a gun turret of the *Collingwood*, he had his first experience of action—in the Battle of Jutland. For his "coolness and courage under fire" he was mentioned in dispatches. Yet characteristically he scarcely alluded to his own part in the battle in a letter which he wrote just afterward to his old tutor. "The men were quite marvelous," he said, and left it at that. All through his life he would give the credit to others rather than himself.

In the summer of 1917 he was forced to leave the Navy after an operation for duodenal ulcer which made a strenuous career at sea out of the question. King George V, habitually stern, but in many ways the most understanding of fathers, realizing perhaps more than anyone his son's disappointment, gave him—as soon as he was well enough to leave hospital—an appointment in the newly formed Royal Air Force. The Prince was on Sir Hugh Trenchard's staff in France when the Armistice was declared. Its immediate effect on his life was his first public mission. He was sent to Brussels to represent King George at the celebrations for the liberation of Belgium. The vast crowds in the streets gave a tremendous reception to the shy slender young man who rode through the city with their own King Albert.

The first post-war year of 1919 brought very little outward change in the life of Lady Elizabeth Bowes-Lyon. She still worked in the hospital, which remained full of wounded right on until the autumn. She formed a local branch of Girl Guides, and organized all their activities; she went to stay from time to time with various friends. She had more responsibilities in her own home too for her sister Rose had married during the war, and Lady Strathmore's health was not good. Very often the nineteen-year-old Elizabeth had to run the entire establishment at Glamis for weeks on end, act as hostess for her father, and deputize for her mother at local functions.

She had even then a natural gift for public speaking, and very often she used to write her father's speeches for him. Many years later both King George VI and her daughters would always consult her over the preparation of their speeches.

"Mummy always puts in such nice little personal touches," Princess Elizabeth once told a friend. "And when she makes a speech herself, she has a way of making you feel that she is talking directly to you."

There was no formal coming-out either for Lady Elizabeth Bowes-Lyon or for any other girls of that war generation. She had already put up her long brown hair into a knot during the previous summer at Glamis, and now the only appreciable difference was that she went up to London more often and began to be seen at social functions. One of them was a dance given by Lord Farquhar for young people. The host was a personal friend of the Royal Family, and two of the King's sons were among the guests. And so it happened that Prince Albert found himself dancing with a girl whose deep blue eyes carried him back over the years.

"Why, I've met you before," he exclaimed. "A long time ago. Wasn't it at a party at Montagu House?" She laughed.

"Yes. You sat next to me. You were eating angel cake."

"And I gave you the cherries off the top."

So simply they took up the threads again; like an interrupted conversation, or the page of a book turned down. And not until long afterward did they even wonder why they should have remembered one another through the years.

The nineteen-twenties came in on a wave of disillusionment. The war was over but in its train it had brought hardship and unemployment. Thousands of demobilized service men were tramping the country looking for jobs. Ex-officers were selling matches in the London streets. In a world without future the common impulse was to live for the moment. So war gratuities were spent recklessly. Night clubs flourished. Even debutantes were seen at them for by now youth had a new slogan—freedom. Chaperones were discarded. A new type of girl had been evolved—cocktail-drinking, hard-smoking, sophisticated, with a mania for sports.

Lady Elizabeth Bowes-Lyon did not conform to the pattern. She went to a great many dances—but she was never seen at a night club, and she neither drank nor smoked. In that era of exaggerated fashions—slit skirts and drooping monkey fur—she dressed simply. Many of her dresses were run up at home by her own maid. She did not even make a cult of sports. She was fond of riding, though she did not hunt. She was a good shot; played a fair game of tennis and an average one of golf, but that was all. Without being old-fashioned, she was un-modern, in the 1920 interpretation of the word.

Perhaps that was one of the reasons why she was outstanding among all the girls of her generation. Everyone who knew her in those days remembers that she was always the center of attraction at any dance and that whenever she went to a house party she always kept the guests in a continuous state of laughter over her mimicry and her absurd sallies—just as her daughter, Princess Margaret, does today.

"There was something irresistible in her personality," one of her oldest friends told me. "She was very witty and full of fun; but you always sensed the kindness and sympathy beneath her gaiety. She had a sort of radiance. Her vitality was so glowing that other women, even though they might be more classically beautiful, seemed insipid beside her."

Her gaiety was one of the things that enchanted Prince Albert. Up till now his life had held duties, responsibilities, hard work, but little enough of fun. By that time he was an undergraduate at Cambridge University, living simply, studying hard—civics, history and geography—riding to lectures on his motor bike, playing tennis with other students. In addition to his normal plan of study, he had already been caught up in the great Industrial Welfare scheme, which was destined to bring him closer to the ordinary working man and woman than any British sovereign in history. He had gone into it at his own wish, and with his usual determination to learn everything that could be learned about the work, he had been gripped by its human interest. Even in those days at Cambridge he was visiting factories and sitting on committees dealing with physical training for industrial workers, summer camps, pensions, canteen planning. His brothers were already beginning to tease him—the Prince of Wales had nicknamed him "The Foreman." But King George was proud of his son's success in this new field. Before he left the University he conferred on him the title of Duke of York.

Away from his desk and his eternal papers he was a very human young man of twenty-five, still sensitive and rather shy, but with a keen sense of humor and a dry, typically British wit. He was completely unaffected, liked to mark the tennis court, roll the lawn, or do little odd jobs in any house where he happened to stay, and still detested more than anything else to be treated with ceremony.

Lady Elizabeth Bowes-Lyon appealed to the youth in him. He found that he could talk simply and naturally to her. Her sense of fun, the light touch which she always brought even to serious moments, delighted him. He had the perception to see that underlying it was a sympathy and a sense of duty as sincere as his own. Even before he paid his first visit to Glamis that autumn he was beginning to be in love with her.

Seeing her in the surroundings of her own home completed the conquest. The atmosphere of Glamis, with its simple friendliness, was after his own heart. He shot over the moors with her brothers and members of the house party; he fished the river Dean with her; he took part in the sing-songs round the piano, and learned the old Scottish ballads.

When he left Glamis he knew that he would never love any other woman, but he waited before asking her to marry him. He was still too uncertain of her answer to take the risk. He realized that, even if she loved him, the decision would not be an easy one for her. Marriage with him would entail heavy responsibilities, a continual round of public duties, a home life shadowed by Royal obligations.

All through that winter and the following year he continued to see her as often as he could. He contrived to get invitations to house parties where he knew she would be a guest. He invited her to tea in his rooms at Buckingham Palace, chaperoned by Princess Mary, who proved a loyal ally. She had paid several visits during the autumn to Glamis—while her brother was a guest there, driving over from Cortachy Castle, where she was staying with Lady Airlie—and she too had fallen under the spell of Lady Elizabeth's charm. It was the beginning of a friendship between two girls which would deepen with the years. Today the

Queen Mother has no more sincere admirer than her sister-in-law.

When Princess Mary married Lord Lascelles it was a foregone conclusion that Lady Elizabeth Bowes-Lyon would be one of the bridesmaids. Many people still remember what a lovely picture she made in her white and silver dress. Just before the wedding she invited the wives of her father's tenants, and members of the staff at St. Paul's Waldenbury, to an informal party to see her bridesmaid's dress. Later—when she became Queen—she introduced the custom of always inviting the staff at Buckingham Palace to see the Royal Family dressed for any special function.

That distant Royal destiny drew nearer to her in the autumn of 1921. All through the summer Lady Strathmore's health had been growing steadily worse. For several weeks she was a semi-invalid with the result that her youngest daughter had to cope with the entire running of the household at Glamis and the entertaining of a long succession of guests. She did it with an ease and efficiency that delighted her father. Even so he had some misgivings when the doctors attending Lady Strathmore insisted on her remaining in bed, for Queen Mary and the Duke of York were expected on a visit and would arrive the next day.

He need not have worried. The twenty-one-year-old Lady Elizabeth was more than equal to the occasion. Queen Mary was charmed, both with the hospitality of Glamis, and with the girl of whom her son had talked so much. The fact that she could deal so calmly and competently with housekeeping on such a scale, and yet find time to entertain her guests and help in nursing her mother, earned the warm admiration of Queen Mary, herself an expert housekeeper.

As she said goodbye the Queen drew her young hostess to her and kissed her affectionately on both cheeks.

Did she, perhaps, in that spontaneous, motherly embrace, feel the shadow of the future?

Chapter 4

At about noon on the 13th of January, 1923, a young man
put away his papers in an orderly pile, closed his desk, and
like thousands of other Londoners, set off for a week end in
the country. As he took the road to Hitchin in his little
sports car anyone noticing him would have been left with
the impression of perfect grooming, humorous gray eyes,
and the type of face which is always called nice rather than
handsome, although it was actually very good looking in a
casual, still boyish way. Not one person in a hundred
would have recognized the Duke of York.

His streamlined sports car ate up the miles to St. Paul's
Waldenbury—like all the King's sons he loved speed and
drove extraordinarily well. And this time there was determination behind his haste. He was on his way to spend the
week end with Lord and Lady Strathmore, and come what
might he was going to persuade their daughter, Lady Elizabeth Bowes-Lyon, to marry him.

He had been a patient wooer for over three years, but
although all their intimate friends knew how deeply he was

in love with her, and believed that he had proposed to her more than once, he had so far made no headway. Now this invitation to visit her home had given him new hope, and he was going to ask her once again.

He had already his parents' blessing. None of the King's sons could marry without first having obtained their father's consent, and this marriage—if it materialized—would be a break from the Hanoverian tradition that a Royal Prince could only take a wife of Royal rank. King George V had swept away a mass of Germanic driftwood during the First World War when he had reverted to the name of Windsor and announced that his sons could take their wives from the three highest ranks of the nobility; but the Duke would be the first to avail himself of the new order of things. He had broached the question to his father at Sandringham soon after Christmas, and been told to go ahead.

"You'll be a very lucky fellow if she says yes," had been the King's comment.

The Duke knew, even before he asked her, that his mother would approve. Queen Mary had never been deceived over her second son. From his nursery days she had recognized the force of his character, so often hidden by diffidence and overshadowed by the more convincing personality of his elder brother. She realized that his was a nature which would essentially respond to love, and that the background of a happy home could be the greatest influence in his life.

At St. Paul's Waldenbury the other mother concerned, Lady Strathmore, was also hoping and praying that her daughter would make the right decision. She knew that Elizabeth was in no hurry to marry, although she had any number of admirers—she had had five proposals within the year. Still she would have to make up her mind sooner or later. Lady Strathmore, who had perception, was fond of the Duke of York, and Queen Mary had pleaded her son's cause with her, but she was too wise to interfere. She waited. Months afterward she wrote to a friend:

> That winter was the first time I have ever known Elizabeth really worried. I think she was torn between her longing to make Bertie happy and her reluctance to take on the big responsibilities which this marriage must bring.

The responsibilities were to be far greater even than the twenty-three-year-old Lady Elizabeth had reckoned, but his need of her won the day. On the Sunday morning after his arrival at St. Paul's Waldenbury, instead of going to church with the rest of the house party, they went for a walk in the wood at the foot of the garden—"The Fairies' Wood" of her childhood—where the first snowdrops were already springing up under their feet. When the family came back from church one look at the radiant faces of the two who had stayed behind told them that all was well.

They were married just over three months later—the 26th of April, 1923, at Westminster Abbey, on a day that dawned with cloudy skies and wet pavements, but had cleared by the time Lady Elizabeth left 17 Bruton Street, which was now her father's London house. The country people from the Glamis estate who had come up for the wedding of "The Lassie" caught the sudden gleam of pale spring sunshine and hailed it as a good omen.

King George caught it too and recorded it in his description of the wedding. "It was rather gray and inclined to rain, but as soon as the bride arrived at the Abbey the sun shone as it always does in her presence," he wrote.

The bluff old King, with his booming quarter-deck voice and his soft heart, had already fallen under the spell of his new daughter-in-law's gift for creating a happy atmosphere—a gift which was to make Princess Elizabeth say years later of her own childhood, "The sun seemed to be always shining."

In spite of the splendid pageantry of the ceremony in Westminster Abbey, the gleaming escorts of cavalry, the brilliant uniforms, there was a note of austerity unusual in a Royal wedding. It was at the wish of the bride and bridegroom. They were being married at a time of black depression, when thousands of families all over the country were undergoing great hardship. Both of them had gained an insight into social conditions—the Duke of York in his work for the Industrial Welfare Society; Lady Elizabeth through helping ex-patients of Glamis to find jobs and dealing with their problems of resettlement. So various economies were made, unostentatiously in the spirit in which years afterward King George VI and Queen Elizabeth would give up many non-essentials in wartime: because their people could not have them. There were no floral decorations at the Abbey, and the bride's trousseau was simple. Much of it was made at home by her own maid. She wore few jewels.

She was followed to the altar, this bride who was the first British subject to marry a Prince in direct succession to the Throne for over two hundred and fifty years, by bridesmaids all British and all commoners like herself. Two of them were her small nieces, Cecilia Lyon and Elizabeth Elphinstone. The rest were all close friends. Miss Diamond

Hardinge, whom she had helped to nurse through a serious
illness the year before in Paris, where her father, Lord Hardinge of Penshurst, was British Ambassador; Miss Betty
Cato, who was to marry her brother Michael Bowes-Lyon
later; Lady Mary Cambridge, Lady Catherine Hamilton,
Lady May Cambridge, Lady Mary Thynne.

They would all—with the exception of Miss Diamond
Hardinge, who died at a tragically early age—remain her
friends through the years, for the Queen Mother has the
Scottish fidelity in friendship. The friends of her childhood
are her friends today. Some of them are quite unknown in
society, but she has kept in touch with them. Even in her
crowded life as Queen Consort she always managed to see
them from time to time, sometimes at small intimate tea
parties at Buckingham Palace, sometimes in their own
homes. Quite often the Royal car has waited outside an unpretentious block of flats or little house in the suburbs.

After a honeymoon which was divided between Polesden Lacey—the lovely house lent to them by Mrs. Ronald
Greville, who was one of Lady Strathmore's oldest friends—
Glamis Castle and Frogmore, the Duke and Duchess
moved into their first home. This was White Lodge in
Richmond Park, one of the King's "grace and favour"
houses. It was a restful, square-built Georgian house, which
had begun its existence as a hunting-box belonging to King
George I and had been enlarged later, first by Queen Caroline, wife of George II, and then by her daughter, Princess
Amelia.

Queen Mary had spent her childhood there, when it
was in the possession of her mother, the Duchess of Teck.
The Queen knew every inch of its sheltered gardens, with

their trim flower beds, broad lawns and lily ponds. She took the greatest pleasure in getting it ready for her son and his bride, while they were on their honeymoon. She paid several visits there and at the last moment added all the little homely touches: arranging vases of the Duchess' favorite roses in her bedroom and filling the cigarette boxes in the study with the Duke's special brand of cigarettes. Even the dogs were not forgotten. Brand new kennels awaited the Duke's setter and the Duchess' golden Labrador.

During the first few months of their marriage the number of their pets increased so much that their accommodation became quite a problem. Several of their friends, knowing their love of animals, were seized with the idea of presenting them with a dog. When the seventh arrived, the Duke and Duchess decided that homes would have to be found for most of them, but as every prospective owner had to be personally known and proved as a dog lover, the process of disposal went very slowly.

The Duchess came back from her honeymoon to a diary already filled with public engagements. All through the summer she opened bazaars and hospital wards, laid foundation stones and visited Industrial Centers with the Duke, in addition to attending all the Court functions. It was an ordeal for a girl who had been born a commoner. She had had no training, as her own daughters would have, in the role of Royalty. They would be spared fatigue by learning to stand for long periods at a time from their earliest childhood; would grow accustomed to crowds and observing eyes as a matter of course. For her there was no gradual process of initiation. After having lived her entire twenty-three years as a private individual, she found herself in a perpetual spotlight. For the first time her life was ruled by a schedule, with every hour planned in advance, and as the months passed there were increasing demands upon her, for as the King's only daughter-in-law in those days there were many engagements which she alone could fill. She worked so hard that the Prince of Wales told her she was doing much more than her share. He was surprised when she answered with complete sincerity, "But I like doing it, David. It's so interesting."

Of course she liked it. She was young, vital, fond of humanity, and endowed with that personal magnetism common to all great artists of the theatre and irresistible when it is found in Royalty. She wanted to please, and she gave pleasure.

King George V was delighted with the freshness of her approach to the routine life of Royalty; with the liveliness which she brought into sedate family gatherings. Her tact could always be relied on to ease any strained situation. She was the first to see a storm threatening and to pour oil on the troubled waters. Her natural sweetness of disposition enabled her—without being colorless—to avoid being involved in any disputes, even though the whole Royal Family confided in her. It did not take them long to discover that she never repeated confidences and that her advice was always worth following. She prevented many a clash between the Prince of Wales and his father.

In King George's eyes she could do no wrong. Once, during the annual ten days when the King held court at Holyrood Palace, the Duke and Duchess of York—through a breakdown of their car which had delayed them in returning from an earlier engagement—were two minutes late for dinner with the King and Queen. When they arrived it was to find the doors of the State dining room already closed.

The Duke, knowing that few things angered his father as much as unpunctuality, was half inclined to forego the dinner and send a suitable excuse afterward, but the Duchess—radiant in a dress of billowing white tulle—quietly led the way into the room and went straight to her place on the King's right.

"I'm so sorry, Papa. I'm afraid we are two minutes late," she began. But the King interrupted her apology with a smile. "No, you are not, my dear," he said. "I think we must have sat down two minutes too early."

For the first few years of their marriage, the Duke and Duchess had no settled home of their own. As the number of their engagements increased they found White Lodge too great a distance from London, and for a time Princess Mary lent them Chesterfield House. From there they carried out a series of visits to Industrial Centers and an official tour of Northern Ireland. There was constant packing and unpacking of trunks by the Duchess' maid, Catherine Maclean—afterward christened "Cata" by Princess Elizabeth, who was responsible for most of the nicknames in the Royal Household.

Cata had entered the Queen Mother's service long before, when she went to Glamis Castle as "young ladies' maid" to the eleven-year-old Lady Elizabeth Bowes-Lyon. She remained with her, first as maid to the Duchess of York and then as Dresser to the Queen, until a few years ago when she was compelled by ill health to resign from her post.

She told me that during that official visit to Northern

Ireland in 1924, the Duke happened to come into the room
one morning when she was packing the Duchess' trunks.

"I should think your back must be nearly broken with
all the stooping over our luggage that you've had to do
lately," he said. "I'm going to put an end to that by getting
you a traveling wardrobe."

He ordered one immediately after they had returned to
London, but as he could not find the type he wanted, he
designed it himself—light-weight, space-saving, and with
accommodation for almost any number of clothes which
could be packed and unpacked without the need for stooping. Queen Mary was so taken with it that she promptly
ordered a similar one, and before long it became the accepted model for the whole Royal Family. Even today the
Queen and Princess Margaret have traveling wardrobes
built on the lines of the one designed by their father. Like
his brother, the Duke of Kent, he had a flair for design
and for engineering and used to carry out all sorts of small
household repairs. He could mend a watch or clock as well
as an expert.

After the heavy program of public duties August came
as a welcome break to both the Duke and Duchess of York.
They spent it every year with their parents; part of the time
with the King and Queen at Balmoral, and the remainder
with Lord and Lady Strathmore at Glamis. During the August of 1924 Queen Mary was concerned to see how tired
her daughter-in-law was looking. King George prescribed a
holiday both for her and for the Duke. The result was a
shooting trip to East Africa which they enjoyed so much
that many years afterward they suggested it in their turn to
their daughter Princess Elizabeth and her husband.

The Duchess, who loves an outdoor life and has never been a town-dweller at heart, revelled in those weeks in the open air; the long marches across rough country; the nights under canvas. She had no fear of the bush, and—thanks to William Fairweather, the head keeper at Glamis, who taught her to shoot as soon as she was old enough to hold a gun—proved to be the best shot of the whole party. Lady Annaly, her lady-in-waiting, and Commander Colin Buist, who was in attendance on the Duke, both remember the number of crocodiles—notoriously difficult to shoot—which she accounted for. She used to say they were the only beasts she could never regret killing!

The trip produced a wonderful collection of photographs of animal life in the bush. Both the Duke and Duchess had made a hobby of photography since their childhood, and they took several cameras with them. Very often they would start off before dawn and spend several hours on the veldt getting pictures of the herds. The collection was to be a joy to their little daughters later, usually as a treat reserved for wet Sunday afternoons.

On the 21st of April, 1926, the baby girl who was destined to become Queen Elizabeth II was born at 17 Bruton Street, Lord Strathmore's London house which had been lent to the young couple. She was a beautiful baby, with her mother's vivid blue eyes and wild-rose skin. In those days, when everyone expected the Prince of Wales to marry, and in any case when her own parents might have sons to stand between her and the Throne, her Royal destiny seemed remote. No future sovereign could have had a less pretentious christening than hers, in the Private Chapel at Buckingham Palace—except perhaps her son Prince Charles twenty-two years later, for by that time the Chapel had been bombed, and the Heir Apparent received his names in the Bow Room at the Palace.

She had just reached the lovable age of eight months and was beginning to develop a firm little personality of her own, when her parents had to leave her for a tour of Australia and New Zealand. The Duchess dreaded the prospect of half a year's separation from her baby, but she had no alternative. The Duke was going on an important mission, to represent King George at the inauguration of the new Australian capital—Canberra, and her presence would be necessary at the various State functions. At least she had the consolation of knowing that no child could be in better hands, for Alah had joyfully reappeared on the scene to take charge of her baby's baby—an older, rather sterner Alah, but still calm and kind and infinitely reassuring. And the grandmothers on both sides were competing for the privilege of putting the respective nurseries of Buckingham Palace and St. Paul's Waldenbury at the new baby's disposal. In the end it was decided that she would spend the first three months of her mother's absence with Lady Strathmore and the next three with Queen Mary.

For the Duke the chief event of the tour was to be the opening of the first Commonwealth Parliament to be held in Canberra. Only the Duchess knew how much he was secretly dreading it, for it would involve his giving an address to a very large audience, and he had never outgrown the speech defect of his childhood. Although he did not stammer in ordinary conversation and could talk interestingly and amusingly on most subjects, he was handicapped as a public speaker.

The story of how he was able to overcome his stammer with the help of Mr. Lionel Logue, the Australian specialist in speech training who was then in London, has often been told. But few people know that it was the Duchess who persuaded him to undergo treatment, or that she herself played an important part in his cure. Every day on the voyage out to Australia she worked with him for at least a couple of hours on the special course of exercises prescribed by Mr. Logue, taking the boredom out of it, making it fun instead of a labor of vowels and consonants. Both of them had their reward when the Duke delivered his first speech in Australia without a trace of hesitation.

When he sat down the Duchess' eyes were shining. She slipped her hand into his, forgetful of those around them. "Darling, it was splendid! I was so proud of you." That little human incident charmed the audience.

This unpretentious Royal couple who referred to each other simply as "my husband" or "my wife" without formalities were very much after the hearts of a young country. The Australians liked their friendliness—the warmth of the Duke's handshake, the way in which the Duchess danced at the Government House Ball in Melbourne with a young and unknown engineer who had been a wartime patient at Glamis hospital. They gave them an enthusiastic welcome at every stage of the tour. This personal popularity was to have a far more important bearing on the future than anyone realized, for at the time of the abdication of King Edward VIII, Australian loyalty would stand solidly behind the new King and Queen.

The Duke's address at the opening of the Canberra Parliament was delivered without any sign of hesitation. He

had overcome his speech defect—as he was to overcome so
many obstacles—by sheer determination. But the fight was
not over, for all through his public life he would have to
put into the preparation of his speeches far more work than
the average speaker. He wrote most of them himself, or at
least drafted them—his sincerity would not let him leave
them to his secretaries—and then he rehearsed them over
and over again. And, as in the days before that first speech
in Australia, he was helped by his wife. Even after he came
to the Throne he used to go through all his most important speeches with her. When he broadcast she was usually
near the microphone where he could see her.

   While the Duke and Duchess were covering the 34,000
miles of their tour of Australia and New Zealand, Princess
Elizabeth was being shared by her two grandmothers. She
started to walk in her mother's old nursery at St. Paul's
Waldenbury, clinging to the big armchair as the first Elizabeth had done. She played with the venerable rocking-horse
and other toys brought out by Alah from the cupboard
where they had lain for twenty years, and made the first of
many friends in the dog world—two large and benevolent
chows belonging to Lady Strathmore. Then she went on to
Buckingham Palace, to give great pleasure to Queen Mary
by producing as her first distinct word "Gan-gan."

   Even then she always had a broad smile of welcome
when her grandmother entered the nursery. Through all
the years that followed there was to be a close bond of affection between them. The baby of those days would grow
from childhood to womanhood watched by the proud and
tender eyes of an old lady, until the time would come when
as Elizabeth II one of the first letters of sympathy which

she would open after her father's death would be signed, in handwriting firm even in sorrow:

> "Your Majesty's most loving grandmother and most dutiful subject,
> Mary R."

King George V frankly doted on his small granddaughter. From having been a strict father apt to be bored by his offspring, he developed into the most indulgent of grandfathers. "Lilibet" exacted as her right all sorts of privileges which his own children had never even dared to ask. Cherished souvenirs of the King's tours and personal possessions which they had only admired from afar were got out for her to play with. During her first Christmas at Sandringham she was still at the crawling stage and could cover the ground at a surprising rate. Members of the Household remember seeing her speeding down the passages on all fours, with the King in hot pursuit.

On a lovely June afternoon in 1927 the Duke and Duchess of York returned to London from their Australian tour and drove straight to Buckingham Palace. Outside the gates a crowd had gathered to welcome them; in the Palace King George was waiting to congratulate his son on the success of his mission. But the Duchess could only wonder whether her baby would have forgotten her. Half a year was a big gap in a total of fourteen months!

Then Lilibet, carefully dressed in her best frock by Alah, who loved great occasions, was brought in. She fixed her mother with a long inquiring stare lasting a few seconds; then suddenly a broad smile of welcome spread over her face and she held out her arms.

Long afterward the Duchess told her daughter how much that recognition had pleased her, and the Princess remembered it when she too became a mother. Every night at Clarence House during the time when the Duke of Edinburgh was away serving with the Mediterranean Fleet, she used to take Prince Charles up to his father's photograph to say, "Good night, Papa" before he went to bed.

"I don't want him to forget his father while he is away and children's memories are so short unless they have something to remind them," the Princess told one of her friends.

Chapter 5

FROM their tour of Australia and New Zealand the Duke and Duchess of York returned to their first permanent home —145 Piccadilly, a large nineteenth-century house facing Hyde Park Corner and backed by the enclosed space of Hamilton Gardens. It was Crown Property and once again Queen Mary played the part of fairy godmother and arranged everything for them—down to the last duster—while they were away.

The house itself was tall, narrow-fronted, rather austere in exterior, but within it was cosy and unpretentious. Essentially a happy home, the home of a young couple very much in love, completely contented in each other and in their little daughter.

Their working week was a full one. The Duke visited factories for the Industrial Welfare Society, ran his Boys' Clubs, and deputized for his father when and where required. The Duchess' program of public duties was so crowded that her lady-in-waiting, Lady Helen Graham, could hardly keep pace with her correspondence.

61

But for both of them the happiest hours of the day began when the last engagements had been fulfilled, when the secretaries had gone, and the big double doors of 145 Piccadilly could close on the outside world. Although they had an immense circle of acquaintances and went out a great deal—both to official functions and to private houses —in the early years of their marriage, they preferred a quiet evening at home to any outside entertainment. To be free to play with their baby in her bath, have a simple dinner together, and sit by the fire talking or listening to the radio, represented a rare pleasure.

Their happiness was proverbial in the Royal Family. The Prince of Wales used to tease his brother over his domesticity. The day was still distant when he would say of him, "He has one matchless blessing . . . not bestowed on me—a happy home with his wife and children."

The household at 145 Piccadilly was a modest one for a Royal establishment. The staff was comparatively small. The Duke had his valet and the Duchess her maid, but they were both independent and liked looking after themselves. The Duke had the Navy's passion for neatness. His bedroom was as spick and span as a ship's locker. Every brush, every stick of shaving soap had its accustomed place; his drawers and cupboards were a model of tidiness.

Both of them were practical in a kitchen and enjoyed getting themselves a meal. In the early days of their marriage, when they went out to a great many evening engagements, they would never allow their servants to sit up for them. They used to let themselves into the house after everyone had gone to bed and steal down to the kitchen to cook kippers or eggs and bacon. Their tastes in food were simple. They enjoyed homely English dishes most of all.

"One of the disadvantages of public life is that people always expect you to like chicken and feed you on it wherever you go," the Duke used to say. He much preferred liver and bacon or herrings fried in oatmeal.

They loved nothing better than to forget for a while that they were Royal. When they traveled, unless it was on an official journey, they took the minimum entourage— usually only a valet, a maid, and the Duke's detective. Lady Granville, the Duchess' sister, still remembers how they came out to Zut one Easter for a short holiday at the cottage which she and her husband had taken on the dunes. As there was no accommodation either for the detective or the chauffeur, they had to be put up at another house some little distance away, and the Duke and Duchess reveled in their freedom until the Belgian authorities discovered their presence and courteously sent a magnificently uniformed and bemedaled *gendarme* to guard them. To the secret dismay of the household he took up his stand at the gate, with his back to the cottage and its tiny patch of garden. Naturally he became an immediate object of interest to passers-by, and all hopes of a really peaceful holiday were beginning to fade when the Duchess went out to the gate and tactfully persuaded him to leave.

The baby Princess Elizabeth started life unburdened by the knowledge of her Royal rank. Both her parents were determined to keep it from her as long as possible, and so bring her up like any other little girl. It was not always easy in London where a crowd collected outside the enclosed space of Hamilton Gardens, to stare at her every time she went out to play. But because no one ever discussed their presence with her, or let her think that it was in any way connected with herself, she accepted it quite naturally. The word "Princess" conveyed nothing to her. Almost as soon as she could talk she had found a name for herself— Lilibet—and everyone called her by it. She learned the usual lessons in humility which every small child has to learn. She discovered that although grown-up people might curtsy to you and sentries might present arms when you appear, you were not absolved from the obligation of being polite to your elders.

Once she was heard by the Duchess talking in a rather self-important way to the clock-winder who used to go every week to 145 Piccadilly to regulate the Duke's collection of eighty-five clocks. Lilibet had always regarded him as a special friend and loved to run round from room to room with him, but she had just entered the phase of superiority which most children go through sooner or later, and was addressing him by his surname without the prefix of "Mister."

Her mother listened to the conversation for a moment and then called softly from outside the door, "Elizabeth," a name which was only used when she was in disgrace.

"Never let me hear you being so rude to anyone again," said the Duchess when her little daughter stood before her. "You know perfectly well that Papa and I never talk to people in that way. Now go back and say that you are sorry."

She went back to the room, very contrite, and held out her hand to the old man: "I'm sorry I was rude and

Inseparable companions always were Elizabeth Bowes-Lyon
and her youngest brother David (The Hon. David Bowes-
Lyon).

Elizabeth and David Bowes-Lyon in the garden of St. Paul's Waldenbury.

Building their house of cards.

Brother and sister with their donkey at Glamis.

Elizabeth, aged six.

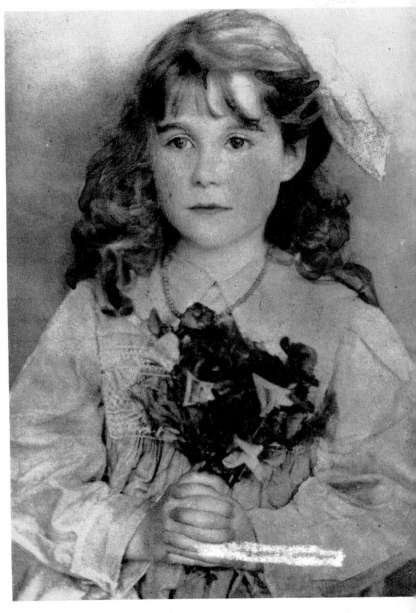

A sketch of the future Queen Mother made by her sister Rose
(now Countess Granville).

Elizabeth on her pony "Bobs."

The little Lady Elizabeth in a costume from the "dressing-up chest" at Glamis.

The family of the Earl and Countess of Strathmore. Elizabeth
is standing next to her mother.

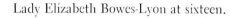

Elizabeth as a schoolgirl at Glamis.   Lady Elizabeth Bowes-Lyon at sixteen.

British Information Services

A shooting party at Glamis the summer before Lady Elizabeth's engagement to the Duke of York (seated at her right in the center of the front row).

Lady Elizabeth at eighteen, the year before her engagement.

International

The Duke and Duchess of York just before their wedding.

Wide World

The Duke and Duchess of York on their wedding day, April
26, 1922.

The Duke and Duchess of York on their honeymoon at
Polesden Lacey.

European

The Duke and Duchess of York on their shooting trip to
East Africa, 1924–1925, with Mr. Felt, the engineer of their
flat-bottomed Nile steamer.

The Duchess of York out-
side their railroad car en
route to Port Sudan.

The Duke of York on the lower reaches of the Nile with a
fine specimen of a Mrs. Gray's Nile Lechwe.

The Duchess of York secures a record head of a white-eared Cob.

Two snapshots of the Duchess of York taken on the shooting
trip to East Africa.

European

The Duchess of York with Queen Elizabeth II in 1926

King George VI and his Queen on the day of their Coronation.

European

The King and Queen with Princesses Elizabeth and Margaret Rose.

British Information Services

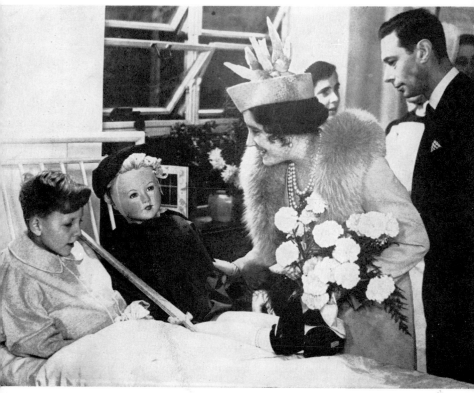

Europea

The King and Queen chat with six-year-old Arthur Barnes in
the Peter Pan Ward of London's Children's Hospital.

didn't mister you," she said earnestly. He was so touched by the apology that he let her wind several clocks.

The nurseries, which occupied practically the whole top floor of 145 Piccadilly and consisted of a suite of rooms opening on to a circular gallery under a big glass dome, formed a little community of their own. It was presided over by Alah—as everyone called her, though she was officially known as Mrs. Knight. She had an under-nurse and a nursery maid to help her; two sisters, Scottish girls from Ross-shire, Margaret and Ruby MacDonald, who joined the household when Princess Elizabeth was a few months old. They remained with the Princesses all through their childhood, and are still with them. Margaret—or "Bobo," as she was nicknamed by the two-year-old Lilibet, when three syllables presented too many difficulties—is now Dresser to the Queen, and Ruby is Princess Margaret's maid.

Pride of place in the sunny day nursery was given to the tall glass-fronted cabinet which contained Princess Elizabeth's particular treasures. Queen Mary had started her, when she was still in her cradle, with a small but perfect collection of china cottages, jade and ivory figures, and birds and animals of all descriptions in blown glass. Every year new pieces were added to it, until she herself became a collector. Today very few people are aware—except the experts who have talked to her—that the young Queen has a connoisseur's knowledge of china and glass.

At the bottom of the cupboard were shelves for toys, later to be shared with Princess Margaret. Every year just before Christmas the two little girls cleared out a lot of them to be sent to hospitals and poor children. They always made the selection themselves: not without occasional pangs of renunciation.

Alah always remembered one year when the Duchess had been reading Princess Elizabeth the story of the Wise Men and their gifts, and had told her that any present given to someone in need was in reality offered to the Christ Child. Lilibet listened with rapt attention, as she always did to any story, but said very little. A few days later when she was getting out her toys for the hospitals Alah was surprised to see her add a new and much prized horse to the pile.

"I suppose I ought to give one of my nicest things to Baby Jesus for his birthday," she explained rather wistfully.

Alah was divided between reluctance to check the spirit of self-sacrifice and anxiety as to what Queen Mary— the donor of the horse—might feel if she discovered that it had been given away!

In spite of her confidence in Alah as the autocrat of her own childhood, the Duchess took charge of her baby's upbringing. Immediately after her return from Australia she set aside certain times of the day for her, and nothing was allowed to interfere with them. All through her own childhood—and right on until her marriage—she had been accustomed to spend an hour in her mother's room before breakfast. She made this an institution in her own home. Every day began for Lilibet with a romp in her parents' room, and ended with playtime in the nursery before bed. Very often the Duchess bathed her herself, with the Duke helping in the process, to the accompaniment of a lot of splashing and shrieks of laughter. Alah, looking on from the doorway, used to shake her head over the pools of water on the floor.

Like many children brought up as the only child in a home for several years, Princess Elizabeth was mentally in advance of her age. At two she could recognize quite a number of tunes when her mother played them on the piano. At three she delighted in using long words and had a funny vocabulary of her own.

Her conversation was a joy to her grandfather King George V. He was proud of her quick mind, her keen observation, and the fearlessness with which she rode her pony. Watching her play with her cousins, Princess Mary's two little boys, George and Gerald Lascelles, the King would laugh to see her taking the initiative in all the games and ordering the two little boys about, although she was the youngest of the three.

"She's a born leader that child," he would say, "a born leader!"

He was always so happy to have her with him that after his serious illness in the winter of 1928 Queen Mary suggested that she should go to keep him company at Bognor where he went to regain his strength. He used to say afterward that going for drives with her and watching her play in the sands did him more good than any medicine.

Lilibet was too young to know the part she had had in her grandfather's recovery, but on the day of the public thanksgiving at Westminster Abbey, Alah let her watch the procession from the windows of her nursery at 145 Piccadilly, and explained the reason for it. She was enthralled with her first glimpse of Royal pageantry.

That night she introduced into her usual bedtime prayers a curious variation of her own.

"Oh, God, I see'd the beautifullest things today," she began, "I see'd the big Scotch soldiers. . . . I see'd the red soldiers. . . . I see'd all the carriages. . . . I see'd Grandpa's gee-gees. . . ."

Here Alah interrupted and tried to recall her to more orthodox petition. But the Princess raised a reproving finger. "Be quiet, Alah. Lilibet's saying her prayers. She's thanking God."

Not until the details of the procession had been enumerated separately—a recital lasting several minutes—would she consent to be tucked up in bed. Alah could never decide whether this private thanksgiving had been inspired by gratitude for the pleasure of the day or a desire to delay bedtime!

Princess Margaret Rose was born on the 21st of August, 1930, at Glamis. The Duke and Duchess had decided months before that the old Scottish Castle which was so dear to them both should be the birthplace of their second child, and by the end of July the whole neighborhood was seething with excitement.

Early in August Mr. J. Clynes, who as Home Secretary was required by ancient custom to be present at the birth of any possible Heir to the Throne, traveled to Glamis. But his stay was a prolonged one for the baby's arrival was not timed according to plan. At the days lengthened to weeks, he grew so afraid of embarrassing the Duchess by his presence that he was almost driven into hiding to avoid meeting her. Fortunately Lady Airlie took pity on him and invited him to stay at Airlie Castle, eight miles away. From there he set out in response to an urgent telephone call from Glamis in the early hours of the morning of August 21st. He reached the Castle to find the new Princess already asleep in her cradle.

But his long vigil had its place in history for many years later, when Princess Elizabeth was expecting her first baby, King George VI decided that the custom of the Home Secretary's official attendance at a Royal birth—originally intended as a precaution against the substitution of some other child—was out of date, and put an end to it.

The new Princess was tiny, with her mother's perfect hands and feet. Lilibet was so unusually solemn when she heard of her arrival that for a moment Alah, who broke the news to her, was afraid that she was jealous and was relieved when she announced: "I shall let her ride Peggy." Peggy was her Shetland pony and most treasured possession. It was a supreme gesture. She had evidently been readjusting her world to her own satisfaction.

From the beginning she adopted a protective attitude toward her little sister. She was naturally an unselfish child, always ready to share her toys and pleasures.

"Oh, let her have it, Alah. She's such a baby," she would say, with the indulgent superiority of her four years' start in life, when Margaret snatched something from her. Later when the baby grew into a sturdy child well able to defend herself she started to discipline her in a firm sisterly fashion.

No childhood could have been happier than that of the curly-haired little girl who spent the first ten years of her life not in the gilt-edged setting of a Court, but in the comfortable home of young and laughter-loving parents.

Whatever triumphs the future may hold for her as Queen, she will never lose the memory of a time when—as she herself said—"The sun seemed to be always shining."

In the eyes of the world the Duke of York was first a conscientious and rather serious-minded young Prince, and then a King with an immense capacity for hard work and self-discipline. As his daughters knew him he was full of fun, good at all kinds of games from tennis to hop-scotch, and addicted to teasing and practical jokes. The Duchess brought the gaiety of her childhood, in a family of ten high-spirited brothers and sisters, to her own home. So parents and children romped and laughed light-heartedly whenever they were alone together, even in the war years when the cares of State lay heavily on the King and Queen.

Lessons began for Lilibet as a game shared with her mother. The Duchess herself taught her to read and started her in a number of general subjects. At five the Princess was beginning to play simple tunes on the piano; she was learning dancing at a little class held every week at 145 Piccadilly, and swimming at the Bath Club. She had been riding since she was four and had already attended her first meet with the Pytchley Hounds.

When the time came for her education to begin in earnest, the Duke of York, remembering his own childhood hedged in by middle-aged tutors, decided to give his daughters as much freedom as possible, and to defy Royal precedent by engaging governesses young enough to be companions as well as teachers. So Miss Marion Crawford, a Scotswoman in her early twenties, was put in charge of the schoolroom.

When it came to the question of French lessons the

Duchess' mind traveled back over the years to the beloved "Madé" of her own childhood. "Madé" was Mme. Guèrin now, and the mother of a grown-up daughter, but they had never lost touch. At least once a month letters were exchanged, and whenever Mme. Guèrin came to London her first visit was to 145 Piccadilly. And so it happened that one afternoon as they stood watching the two little Princesses playing in Hamilton Gardens the Duchess slipped her hand through her old governess' arm.

"Madé darling," she said, "I've just been thinking how nice it would be if your daughter came to mine."

So after that Georgina Guèrin joined the family and at holiday times traveled up with the children to Sandringham in the winter and Scotland in the summer.

The holiday in Scotland was the high spot of the year for the whole family. To the Duke and Duchess it meant a respite from crowds and formalities; blank pages in an over-full engagement book; long days out of doors. The children looked forward for weeks ahead to the visit to their grandparents, Lord and Lady Strathmore. Glamis was as much a child's paradise to them as it had been to their mother. They played Red Indians in the woods and picnicked on Hunter's Hill, as she had done; they raided the stillroom for biscuits hot from the oven, and coaxed crystallized cherries and slabs of plain chocolate from the same cook. They spent their pocket money on toffee and peppermint humbugs at the village shop, and watched the trains go out at the local station. And when the evenings grew too cold for playing in the garden, they ransacked the dressing-up chests or got out the battered scrap-books that had amused generations of Bowes-Lyon children.

The great event of the month was Princess Margaret's birthday, for there was always chicken and ice cream for lunch and a party with a dazzling array of cakes made by the staff who worshipped her. The entire neighborhood always regarded her as their own Princess, born among them, on Scottish soil.

Both the Princesses have always had their mother's deep affection for Scotland. The first songs they learned were the old Scottish ballads which the little Elizabeth Bowes-Lyon had sung in her childhood; they too were imbued with Jacobite sympathies. This sometimes resulted in a conflict of loyalties. An old friend of the Royal Family still remembers how King George VI laughed over a discussion between Princess Elizabeth—who was then just beginning to study history—and a small guest who had come to tea.

The two children were talking of the '45 when suddenly Princess Elizabeth burst out indignantly, "You're *not* to call him 'The Pretender.' "

"But what am I to call him, Lilibet? I can't say 'The King,' " protested the guest, a forthright and logical child.

Princess Elizabeth shot a quick glance at her father and her sensitive little face flushed. It was plain that this aspect had not occurred to her.

"No, of course you can't," she said loyally. "But any way you could say 'Prince Charles.' "

And today the Heir Apparent to the Throne of England bears the name of the last Stuart Prince!

From Glamis the little girls and their parents went on to Birkhall, the small eighteenth-century house near Ballater which King George put at the disposal of the Duke and Duchess every summer. Here there was more of the holiday spirit than in any of the other Royal residences. While the Duke went deer-stalking, the Duchess and Mlle. Guèrin used to go for walks with the children along the moss-covered banks of the river Muick, very often taking a picnic tea with them in a basket tucked into the pram provided for Princess Margaret who was apt to tire on the return journey.

Georgina Guèrin—now Mme. Reinold—told me that some of her most vivid memories are of those autumn walks through the yellow and scarlet woods, with the young Duchess, very pretty and glowing in her country tweeds, pushing Margaret in her pram. Very often she would tell her children as they went along a fairy tale of the woods. She told it so dramatically and with such a wealth of fantasy that the little girls were always enthralled, and even Mlle. Guèrin found herself waiting for the continuation.

When the trees were glistening with the first frosts they returned to London; the Duke and Duchess to a long program of engagements; the children to the familiar nursery of 145 Piccadilly, lessons and—as a great treat—an occasional party. Both of them were good mixers from their babyhood and loved parties, but they were not allowed too many of them.

At one party, given by Lady Louis Mountbatten at Brook House in Park Lane, Princess Elizabeth met a little boy whose hair was even fairer than her own. His name was Prince Philip of Greece and he was already entered for a preparatory school in Cheam. They played together, and sat side by side at tea, but years were to pass before their next meeting.

So, by a funny coincidence, Queen Elizabeth II met her husband just as her mother had done, at a children's party when she was five and he was ten. But the end of that meeting was not so idyllic, for instead of parting with tender memories, Princess Elizabeth and Prince Philip quarrelled over the privilege of pressing the elevator button on the way down from the penthouse at Brook House, and were led away by their respective nannies glaring furiously at one another!

Chapter **6**

Life had begun very differently for the little boy whose name was Philip, Prince of Greece and Denmark.

There had been tremendous rejoicings when he was born to Princess Alice, beautiful English wife of Prince Andrew, son of King George I of Greece. Four elder sisters had preceded him into the world, and a son and heir had long been awaited.

No child could have had a lovelier birthplace than the family home on the Greek island of Corfu, a rambling villa set like a jewel among deep cypress and olive groves, and surrounded by gardens stretching down to the sea.

But the boy who was born there on a June night in 1921, when the air was heavy with the scent of pine and eucalyptus and a thousand blended flowers, and the song of the nightingales contended with the gentle lapping of the waves, was never to know its beauty. Before he was out of his cradle the future changed dramatically for him.

Philip's grandfather, King George I of Greece, a Prince of Denmark before he accepted the Crown of the Hellenes,

91

was a staunch admirer of England and proud of the fact that his favorite sister, Alexandra, was the beloved Queen Consort of King Edward VII. All his children were reared in the English way of life by nurses and tutors brought out from England.

Prince Andrew, King George's fourth son, strengthened the bond by marrying an English princess, Alice of Battenburg, daughter of the sailor Prince Louis of Battenburg, who became the first Marquess of Milford Haven, a distinguished British Admiral; and changed the family name during the First World War to Mountbatten.

Like his four older sisters—the Princesses Margareta, Theodora, Cecile and Sophie—Philip was fair, with the clean-cut features of his father's Danish ancestry and the clear blue eyes of his mother's family, the Mountbattens.

The heritage King George I of Greece bequeathed to his descendants, when he met his death at the hands of an assassin in 1913, was a troubled one. Within the next ten years the Royal Family was twice driven out of the country by its rebellious subjects.

The baby Prince Philip was born during an uneasy lull between two political upheavals. His uncle, King Constantine, had been recalled only a few months before to the kingdom from which he was expelled in 1917. There were scenes of frenzied enthusiasm in Athens when he returned with the rest of the Royal House, including Prince Andrew and Princess Alice. But the rejoicing was short-lived. Greece was involved in a disastrous war with Turkey which ended in the massacre of thousands of Greek troops and civilians at Smyrna. A scapegoat had to be found for popular indignation, and the King was the most convenient victim. Insurrection broke out in the army and spread through the whole country. Civil war was averted only by the news of King Constantine's abdication.

The entire Royal Family shared his disgrace, but most of the blame fell on Prince Andrew, who had commanded an army corps in the Asia Minor campaign. He was arrested, kept in solitary confinement, and finally tried on a charge of military incompetence. For days his life hung by a thread. Everyone expected that he would be shot.

In a last desperate effort to save her husband, Princess Alice appealed to her English relatives. King George V took up the cause immediately and sent his emissary to Greece. As a result of the pressure he brought to bear on the new Government, the death sentence on Prince Andrew was commuted at the last moment to banishment. A British destroyer put in at Piraeus, the port of Athens, to take him and his wife and children away to safety.

The baby Prince Philip, brought with his sisters from the villa at Corfu to embark with his parents at Athens, knew nothing of those days of suspense, or of the family's rescue. He played with the sailors, slept in a cradle improvised from an orange box, and made great friends with the ship's cat. It was only afterward that Princess Alice remembered that her son had walked his first few steps alone on the deck of a British warship.

The Republican Government set up in Greece issued a decree deposing the entire Royal House, forbidding any of its members to enter the country again on pain of death, and confiscating all their private property. Like the rest of the Royal Family, Prince Andrew and his wife and children were now stateless, homeless and almost penniless. They decided to settle in France.

Prince Andrew had many friends in and around Paris, including his French sister-in-law, Princess Marie Bonaparte, wife of his brother Prince George, who owned extensive property at St. Cloud. She offered the family one of the villas on her estate, where living would be cheaper than in England, a serious consideration with four daughters to be launched in the world and a baby son to be educated. So after a few weeks at a hotel in Paris, the family moved into an unpretentious villa in the rue du Mont Valérien, St. Cloud.

The fact that he had no real home of his own did not worry Philip in those early days, for he was a merry, essentially practical child, with a gift for adapting himself to his surroundings, and a great sense of humor.

The presiding deity of his childhood was his English nurse Miss Roose—or "Roosie" as they all called her—who had given her affections to Princess Alice when she was a nursemaid in the service of an English family with whom the golden-haired Princess stayed as a child of thirteen. One evening when the nursemaid was brushing her hair the Princess said impulsively:

"Roosie, when I grow up and get married, will you come and live with me for always?"

Roosie promised, and then thought no more about it until years later she received a letter from Princess Alice, then Princess of Greece, with an invitation to come out to Athens to take charge of her first baby.

So Roosie, by then middle-aged, gave up a safe job in the household of an American millionaire, and embarked on a new life in Greece. In an incredibly short time she had the nursery running on English lines. Each succeeding baby was reared on English baby food, dressed in woollies sent out from a London store, and rocked to sleep to the music of English nursery rhymes.

This early background, allied to the fact that their mother was English, had an immense influence on Philip and his sisters. Although none of them ever spent more than a few isolated days in England in those first years, all five were British in appearance and in their way of life.

Philip especially took after his mother. Even as a child the Mountbatten strain was dominant in him. He had their fearlessness and independence. He was devoid of inhibitions and did not know the meaning of self-consciousness.

Miss Roose used to tell the story of the day when he was taken, at the age of three, to a children's party given by Queen Mary. All the other little guests were slightly over-awed by the occasion as they waited sedately to be presented to the Queen. When it came to Philip's turn he appeared before her barefooted, carrying his shoes and socks in one hand.

"Why not?" he said in answer to Roosie's shocked protests. "My feet were hot. The Queen must know feet get hot sometimes."

He never met his mother's father, the first Marquess of Milford Haven, for the Admiral died only a few weeks after the birth of his grandson. It was a pity, for they had much in common. The sailor who was born a Prince of Battenburg and won his way inch by inch, in the face of British prejudice against a foreigner, to the post of First Sea Lord, would have been proud of a grandson who would one day renounce his status as a Prince of Greece and Denmark to become plain Lieutenant Mountbatten of the Royal Navy.

Linking the two together was the seafaring tradition of the Mountbattens. Both the Admiral's sons followed in their father's footsteps and entered the service. The elder— the second Marquess—constituted himself as Philip's guardian in those days of exile, kept him in pocket money, and lost no time in entering him for an English preparatory school.

But it was the Admiral's younger son, Lord Louis Mountbatten, who had first place in his little nephew's imagination. Rich, handsome, debonair, he used to flash across the gray horizon of the exiles at St. Cloud, bringing with him an atmosphere of excitement—of journeys, ships and high-powered cars.

The walls of Philip's bedroom were covered with photos of "Dickie," as everyone called him—Dickie in naval uniform, Dickie playing polo, Dickie at the helm of a yacht.

His four sisters being much older than himself, Philip soon learned to be independent and to rely on his own company. He used to dress and undress himself almost as soon as he could walk, wrestling unaided with buttons and shoelaces until he had mastered them.

Although the household was run on strictly economical lines, and with a small staff, there was often barely enough money for actual necessities.

To ease the financial situation, Princess Alice opened a shop in the fashionable rue St. Honoré in Paris, where she sold embroideries, tapestries and antiques. Her two eldest daughters, the Princesses Margareta and Theodora, acted as saleswomen. Americans, flocking to Paris in great numbers in those early nineteen-twenties, liked the thrill of being served by royalty in exile, and the venture succeeded.

"Hellas," as the shop was called, absorbed the energies of Princess Alice and her two eldest daughters; the two youngest, the Princesses Cecile and Sophie, were still in the schoolroom; so until he grew old enough to begin lessons, Philip was left to his own devices.

He was never at a loss for something to do. He had a burning energy in those days. He saved up his pocket money month by month until at the end of two years he had enough to buy a secondhand bicycle; on that, he used to career all through the grounds of Princess Bonaparte's estate, and beyond along the roads of St. Cloud.

Although he was the baby of the family he was more than capable of holding his own in the world. Other children, deceived by his sunny smile and angelic blue eyes, were surprised to find him tough. One day he came in from the beach with a cut on his lip and one eye nearly closed after a fight with a French boy. Miss Roose clucked like a frightened hen.

"He said England and Greece were both rotten countries," Philip explained briefly. "I made him take it back."

"But, Philip, he has blacked your eye," lamented Miss Roose.

"Well, I blacked both his," the champion retorted with satisfaction.

Prince Philip was six when he went to his first school—
"The Country Day and Boarding School" at St. Cloud, run
by Donald MacJannett, an American and a graduate of
Tufts College, Massachusetts.

The other pupils, most of them the children of American diplomats and businessmen in Paris, were curious about
the new boy who was a Prince, and very much on the
watch for any signs of conceit. They need not have worried.
The one thing Philip most wanted to forget was his Royal
descent. His teachers found him not outstanding in any
way; just a nice, ordinary little boy, good-tempered and re-
liable, always ready to wipe the blackboard after lessons or
put the books away.

In the year 1932 all his sisters married, one after the
other. All four bridegrooms were German princes. Although
that fact seemed of little importance then, when the name
of Adolf Hitler was only that of a party leader, later, during
the war, it was to mean the complete breakup of the family.
But it had an immediate effect on Philip's life. The marriage of his second sister, Princess Theodora, to the young
Markgrave Berthold of Baden, was to change the course of
his life.

Princess Theodora's husband succeeded to the title of
Markgrave of Baden only three years before his marriage,
on the death of his father, Prince Max, Germany's last
chancellor under the imperial regime. With it he inherited
a magnificent old castle at Salem, on the shores of Lake
Constance, and an ideal.

Prince Max had been a philanthropist whose keen interest in education led him to found in one of the wings
of his own castle a school run on progressive lines. The

headmaster was a young German, Kurt Hahn, who had studied at Christ Church College, Oxford, and spent much of his life in Britain.

The system of education at Salem was based on principles which were revolutionary in that Germany of cast-iron class distinctions. Its keynote was the equality of all men; its aim self-discovery and the development of imagination and initiative. The pupils included children of the greatest families in Europe and children of small farmers and tradespeople. Fees were fixed according to the income of the parents.

When Princess Theodora of Greece became the Markgravine of Baden in 1932, the school had expanded from the original handful of local children to over four hundred boys and girls, and more and more of the castle and of the surrounding estate had been given over to it.

Prince Berthold, who regarded it as a trust from his father, became, in his turn, absorbed in the scheme, and before long his wife was sharing his enthusiasm. Prince Philip, spending the Easter holidays with his sister, found the whole household intent on school affairs.

By that time he was in his third year at Cheam, the three-centuries-old English preparatory school which his uncle, the Marquess of Milford Haven, had chosen for him. Philip liked the school, although he showed no outstanding ability there. His only claim to distinction was his sports record. He kept goal for the first eleven at soccer, played for the first fifteen at rugby, and was in the cricket eleven. He also won the diving competition in his last term, and made the school's record high jump.

By now he was beginning to think of the Navy as a

career. All the Mountbattens were sailors. His cousin, Lord
Medina, had left Cheam to go directly to Dartmouth. He
might well have done the same, but for his visit to Salem.

He loved the life there; the excursions into the forest
and on the lake, the sports that were new to him, such as
wrestling and javelin-throwing, the mixing with boys and
girls of all nationalities. He wrote to the Marquess of Milford Haven, who had been appointed by his father as his
guardian, saying that he would like to enter Salem. He
went there the following year.

Although Prince Philip was at Salem less than two
years, the school left its imprint on him. The coeducational
system freed him from the shyness of the average schoolboy, and he could talk easily to girls without any embarrass-
ment. It was almost certainly this poise that put Princess
Elizabeth at her ease in the early days of their friendship.
He slipped naturally into a brotherly relationship with her,
and his casual unaffected friendliness came as a refreshing
change in her sheltered life as Heir to the Throne.

He still believes in coeducation. When Princess Anne
was born he was highly delighted to have "one of each."

"Charles needs the companionship of a sister," he
said. "Boys and girls ought to be brought up together."

Like the rest of Germany, Salem felt the heel of the
Nazi jackboot. The humanitarian Prince Max of Baden,
who had worked tirelessly for the relief of British prisoners
in Germany during the First World War, had had a
maxim: "To love your enemy is the sign of those who remain loyal to the Lord even in time of war." He had passed
on his principles to his son. Although the school eventually
came under SS control, its spirit was never extinguished.

Immediately after the first Nazi murders, Kurt Hahn, the headmaster, sent out a circular letter to all old boys of the school, telling them to choose between the teachings of Salem and those of Hitler. It was a courageous act, and one that might have had worse consequences than it did; as it was, when a copy fell into the hands of the Nazis, Hahn was arrested and thrown into prison.

Meanwhile the thirteen-year-old Prince Philip evolved a line of opposition all his own. Wherever he was, in the school, or in any public place, he refused to give the Nazi salute. What was more, whenever he saw it given by others he doubled up in laughter.

Only the pompous, crippled Nazi mentality could be seriously perturbed by a schoolboy's ridicule, but Philip was dealing with Nazis, and he was not simply a schoolboy, but brother-in-law of the influential Markgrave of Baden.

His defiance was ill-timed too, for Hitler was making an all-out bid to win over the youth of Germany. Thanks to Philip's example, a hard core of dogged resistance was beginning to form at Salem.

So there were representations to the Markgravine that something must be done about her young brother; he must conform to the movement or go. Princess Theodora wrote to friends in England, asking them to send for Philip.

"He is really endangering himself and us," she wrote. "He will have to go away somewhere to safety."

He went away to Gordonstoun, near Elgin in Scotland, where by this time Kurt Hahn was running a boys' school on the same lines as Salem. Largely through the intervention of British friends the schoolmaster had been released from prison, and allowed to leave Germany.

Hahn's choice of Scotland was deliberate. Many years
before, when a student at Oxford, he went to Morayshire
to recover from a serious illness, and was drawn to the wild
beauty of the countryside and still more to the people;
among the farmers and fisherfolk he made lifelong friends.

So when he returned years later, Scotland was the
natural choice for the type of school he had in mind. Its
rugged sea coast, mountains and rivers were the perfect
setting for the athletics and seamanship he planned to
teach; the democracy engrained in the Scottish character—
the spirit of "a man's a man for a' that" which enables the
laird and his gillie to work side by side—was the living example of the Salem precept: "Free the sons of the rich
and powerful from the enervating sense of privilege."

The influence of Gordonstoun—particularly that of
Kurt Hahn, its headmaster—has been one of the strongest
factors in Prince Philip's life. In those impressionable years
of adolescence it moulded his character; it is reflected even
today in his approach to the routine role of Royalty.

The aim of the school was—and still is, for Gordonstoun has expanded considerably since Philip went there
in 1934 as one of its first pupils—to develop independence
of thought and imagination, a sense of responsibility and
self-effacement in a common cause. Academic success is
considered of less importance than equipping boys, who
come from widely different social backgrounds, for the full
enjoyment of life.

The school program is divided between intellectual
studies, athletics (with more emphasis on seamanship, riding, hurdling and javelin-throwing than on team games)

and practical work, which can be anything from road-mending and hut-building to gardening and carpentry.

Physically it is a toughening regime. Prince Philip, like the rest of the school, began every day, summer and winter, with an ice-cold shower and a half-mile run before breakfast. Several times a week, in all weathers, he walked or cycled the three miles to the little harbor at Hopeman for practical seamanship. It was a proud day when he and several other boys finished building the school's first boat, and a still prouder one when they were allowed to try her out on the Moray Firth.

Like everyone else at Gordonstoun he did his share of the household chores—made beds, polished lockers, and pumped water for his housemaster's bath. When the headmaster had guests, if it happened to be his particular duty, he waited on them at meals, carried their luggage up to their rooms, and did anything else that was required. The mother of one of the masters, who stayed a few days at the school, still remembers how efficiently he used to clean her shoes.

He learned to tackle cheerfully and capably a variety of jobs indispensable in any community but not usually associated with the life of a Royal prince.

"Could I have a look at the pigsty?" was his first request when he paid a visit to Gordonstoun in the summer of 1949. He examined it with a critical eye. "I helped to build it, and I wondered whether it was still standing," he explained.

In those school years his main interest was athletics, and so he excelled at almost all sports. He was the best hurdler and javelin-thrower in the school, was in the first eleven at hockey, and in the rugby fifteen. At cricket he captained the first eleven.

He was probably the best sailor the school had. On cruises to Norway and along the west coast of Scotland, he spent most of his time in the galley in rough weather—for the simple reason that he was the only member of the crew who could be relied upon not to be seasick. He learned to cook that way. He still prides himself on being able to fry sausages and bacon or make a beefsteak pudding.

The sea was his passion. Whenever he could find an excuse he was down at the little windswept fishing village of Hopeman, talking to the fishermen at the harbor, helping them to bring in their catches, or clean their boats.

"Philip just couldn't go wrong with cars or a sail," Alexander Findlay, the boatbuilder who has made boats for three generations of Hopeman fishermen, says. "The first time he worked in my yard I knew yon would be a lad you could trust with the helm of a boat, and I was right."

When he left Gordonstoun in the spring of 1939 Prince Philip was head boy—or guardian, as they call it—of the school. He was also captain of the Coastguard Watchers (a special branch of H.M. Coastguard Service in which the senior boys of Gordonstoun were enrolled) and an instructor under the Moray Badge scheme, training local boys in athletics.

In four and a half years he had changed from a wild coltish child, self-willed and impatient of all authority, into a responsible boy with a capacity for leadership and—to quote his headmaster, Kurt Hahn—"the highest sense of service of all the boys in the school."

The wider experiences of his schooldays—working on

the Gordonstoun estate, in the hayfields of the neighboring farmers, or the smithy of the village blacksmith; sharing the coastguards' watch on a stormy night—had admitted him to a world normally barred to Royalty. From fishermen and farmers he learned lessons not to be found in books. But he had still to discover himself.

Kurt Hahn realized that he was as yet only at the crossroads. In his final report he wrote: "Prince Philip is a born leader, but he will need the exacting demands of a great service to do justice to himself. His best is outstanding; his second best is not good enough. . . . His gifts would run to waste if, in later life, he were not forced to tap his hidden reserves."

Chapter 7

In May 1935 King George V and Queen Mary celebrated their Silver Jubilee. Thousands of people lined the streets for the Royal Procession to St. Paul's Cathedral; a dense mass waited outside Buckingham Palace to watch the start.

In the first carriage to swing out of the gates sat the Duke and Duchess of York and their children. The eyes of the crowd took in the slim good-looking young man in the uniform of an Admiral of the Fleet; the pretty wife beside him; the two little girls opposite, flower-like in summer silks and daisy-wreathed hats. As two white-gloved hands were waved—palms inward in careful imitation of their mother—to acknowledge the cheers of the crowd, a man's voice rang out suddenly above all the rest. "There goes the hope of England." The first murmur of assent swelled into a roar of applause as the procession went on its way.

The crowd forgot—after the fashion of crowds—for there were still eighteen months to go before the limelight of publicity would catch up with the occupants of that carriage.

106

To the nation as a whole the Duke and Duchess of York were in those days a conscientious young couple, carrying out a variety of public duties in a quiet, unspectacular way, without a tenth part of the build-up given to the Prince of Wales. The Duke was known to thousands of schoolboys for his Summer Camps, where boys of all classes—from public schools and back streets of industrial towns—met on an equal footing to spend a holiday under canvas every year. The Duchess was known for her work for housing and child welfare, for her famous smile, and, most of all, as the mother of the two best-loved children in the country.

In that Jubilee year of 1935 she had more time to spare for her home, for now the King had two other daughters-in-law to share the burden of public duties. Prince George, the Duke of Kent, had been the next to marry. His bride, the beautiful Princess Marina of Greece, had brought the glamour of her great-aunt Queen Alexandria into the Royal Family again. And the next year the Duke of Gloucester had married Lady Alice Scott, the daughter of the Duke of Buccleuch.

Princess Elizabeth had been a bridesmaid at both weddings. Her little white sleeveless frocks with their full ballerina skirts had set a fashion for children's parties for years to come. The Duchess of York, who always chose all her daughters' clothes herself, had revolutionary ideas in those days when most children were over-dressed. The Princesses were the first to wear sensible printed cotton frocks in summer, and plainly cut streamline coats in winter. They scarcely ever appeared in hats except on the most formal occasions. Other mothers, seeing their photos in the press, followed suit and before long all the children in Kensington Gardens were hatless.

The Duke and Duchess spent most week ends with their little daughters at Royal Lodge in Windsor Great Park, which the King had given them as a country house. They were fonder of this home than any other, for it was the only one of their own creation, with furniture and decorations chosen by themselves, and fittings made to the Duke's own design. There was little or nothing of a Royal residence about the building, which dated from Regency days. It was just a comfortable country house, with a happy lived-in atmosphere. In the years to come it was to represent to the whole family a refuge from the formalities of Court life, a place within easy reach of London where they could relax, get into country clothes and trim the lawn or bathe the dogs.

There was always a colony of dogs of various breeds—corgis predominating—following the household from one residence to another. In addition to these there were the Princesses' own pets which ranged from two shy little fawns to rabbits and white mice. Both of them had inherited their mother's love of animals. Any lean stray cat was sure of a comforting supper at 145 Piccadilly, for the Duchess of York always put saucers of milk and scraps outside the windows at night. In the end so many cats used to congregate round the doors that Alah got quite worried over the possibility of their bringing germs to the house, but neither the Duke nor the Duchess would hear of their being driven away, and the mere suggestion roused a storm of protest from the little Princesses.

In those pre-war days both the Duke and Duchess

were keen tennis players, and often spent most of the week ends at Royal Lodge on the new hard court which they had laid down. They generally managed to fit in a round or two of golf as well, although the Duchess never cared very much for the game. The little girls went riding in Windsor Great Park most mornings with their father and passed many happy afternoons playing housekeeping in "The Little House"—the wonderful miniature Welsh cottage given to Princess Elizabeth by the people of Wales—which was an unending joy to both of them.

Sunday mornings at Royal Lodge bore the imprint of the Duchess' childhood at Glamis, for after breakfast she told her daughters Bible stories and taught them the psalms which she had learned from her own mother. She always had the list of hymns for the day sent to her by the chaplain and before the family started for church she used to play them over on the piano while the little girls sang them with their father. To this day both the Queen and Princess Margaret know a surprising number of hymns by heart. Their favorite in those early years was the rousing tune of "Onward Christian Soldiers" which lent itself to marching round the room.

Church was followed by family lunch to which Princess Elizabeth—and Princess Margaret when she was old enough—always came down. In the evening, before they went to bed, there were hilarious games of Snap and Rummy with their parents. It was just the ordinary happy week end of thousands of middle-class families all over Britain; except that it was lived within the shadow of a Throne.

To the entire younger generation of the Royal Family,

Royal Lodge was a second home. Scarcely a week end passed without one or another of the King's sons dropping in for tea. The Prince of Wales would stop on his way to Fort Belvedere, his country house near Windsor, sometimes alone, sometimes with friends. The Duchess of Kent would drive over from Coppins with her baby son, to the great delight of the two Princesses, who loved to take him to "The Little House" to lend realism to their favorite game of "fathers and mothers." Both of them were devoted to their beautiful Aunt Marina, and Princess Margaret especially had an unbounded admiration for her.

"I *should* so like to have that kind of face," she would sigh to Alah, and the old nurse, who never encouraged vanity, would retort briskly, "There would be nothing wrong with your own if you would stop looking at it so often in the glass."

The whole Royal Family met at Sandringham for the Christmas of 1935. There were all the usual festivities but the King looked haggard and ill. He pulled crackers with his two little granddaughters and watched them open their presents, but he was only the shadow of his former self.

He had arranged to go with Queen Mary and the rest of the family—including the two Princesses—to take tea a few days after Christmas with some old friends in the neighborhood, but at the last moment he did not feel well enough and decided to remain behind. He refused to have anyone stay to keep him company except Princess Elizabeth.

The King and the little girl spent the whole afternoon together. They walked in the gardens, in the first pale January sunshine, and then Lilibet ran upstairs and changed proudly into her new dress to pour out tea for her grandfather. After that she brought out her games. They were so engrossed in a picture puzzle that they did not even hear the return of the family, until Queen Mary came into the room and asked the King whether he had been bored.

"Bored?" he echoed. "I've had one of the happiest afternoons I think I ever had in my life with Lilibet as my hostess."

It was the last time she would be able to give pleasure to her grandfather. Less than a fortnight afterward, as the two Princesses were adding the finishing touches to a big snow man which they had made in the gardens at Sandringham, Queen Mary came out of the house and told them gently that the King was very ill and that they were to go back to London that afternoon. They followed her toward the house, awed into silence by the news, but as she turned to leave the garden Princess Elizabeth, with the instinctive delicacy of childhood, took her spade and leveled the snow man to the ground.

A few days later she stood, holding her mother's hand in St. George's Chapel, Windsor, and watched the King's coffin lowered into the Royal vault. The tears which trickled down her cheeks, in spite of her self-control, were for the loss of a loved grandfather. She was too young to realize that this was the passing not only of a Sovereign but of an epoch.

For the first six months of the new reign it seemed that there would be few changes for the Duke and Duchess of York. The Duke was already beginning to deputize for his brother, King Edward VIII, as he had done for his father, and his activities were extending into wider fields. There was some talk of a colonial governorship for him, but nothing would be decided until after the Coronation, which was fixed for the following year—the 12th of May, 1937.

In the early autumn of 1936, while the Duke and Duchess were spending their usual holiday with their children at Birkhall, while ten-year-old Princess Elizabeth was landing her first salmon with her mother's help, and six-year-old Princess Margaret was terrifying Alah by riding her pony without a leading rein; while the press was full of plans for the forthcoming Coronation and steamship offices all over the world were being besieged for bookings; while new Edward VIII stamps were being issued and new coinage was being minted, the first breeze of rumor arose coupling the King's name with that of Mrs. Wallis Simpson. Through the winter months it gradually gained volume until it became a certainty early in December when the whole nation was stunned by the news of the deadlock between the King and his Ministers.

The human drama of that fateful week of constitutional crisis was dominated by the tragic figure of the King, faced with the choice between his Throne and the woman he loved. Very little public sympathy was expended upon the less romantic younger brother who had so often deputized for the King in his unassuming way, and who would now have the burden of kingship thrust upon him. Yet his was perhaps the greater renunciation. Nothing was dearer to him and the home-loving Scottish girl he had married than the simplicity of their private life, and now that lay in the balance against duty. Night after night the Duke drove out to Fort Belvedere in an attempt to prevail on his brother not to abdicate.

In the meantime the Duchess lay ill at 145 Piccadilly with a severe attack of tonsillitis. Outside the house crowds surged every evening, arguing and shouting. The cry "We want King Edward!" rang out repeatedly, followed by angry murmurs. The voices reached her as she lay in bed, unable to sleep, quietly reading her Bible. Her maid Cata Maclean noticed that the Duchess always turned that week to the fourteenth chapter of St. John's Gospel: "Let not your heart be troubled."

"I never realized how comforting it was until now," she told Cata.

On the afternoon of December 10, Queen Mary went to her daughter-in-law, putting on one side her personal sorrow to give help and comfort. For by now the suspense was over; King Edward VIII had signed the Instrument of Abdication that morning. The younger brother who had wished least of all things to wear a crown had succeeded him. And the Lady Elizabeth Bowes-Lyon who had once hesitated to take on the responsibilities of marriage with a younger son of the Royal House had become Queen.

Perhaps Queen Mary understood more than anyone else the sacrifices that would be demanded of this young couple, who had been so happy in their unpretentious home life, for she remained nearly two hours with her daughter-in-law, while snowflakes fell lightly over Piccadilly, and upstairs in the nursery a ten-year-old girl played with her little sister, not knowing that the future had been changed for her.

Going back to Marlborough House Queen Mary wrote in her own hand that courageous message, commending to the nation the new King, her second son, and "my dear

daughter-in-law who will be his Queen. May she receive
the unfailing trust and affection which you have given me
for six-and-twenty years," she wrote. "I know that you have
already taken her children to your hearts."

She had unerringly touched the right chord. The people, bewildered and bitterly disillusioned, were divided in
loyalty to the new Sovereign, but the little Princesses were
familiar national figures.

There were only a few sightseers lingering round the
doors of 145 Piccadilly on the evening of December 12
when the new King took his daughters with him to see the
picturesque Proclamation Ceremony at St. James's Palace,
but when the rumor spread that they would be returning, a
crowd of twenty thousand gathered to wait for them. When
at last the car drove up and the two little girls tumbled out
—sleepy but still smiling, and very interested in the sea of
faces around them—a roar of cheering broke out. Perhaps
the conviction spread through all those thousands that this
nice-looking young man, so unaffected, so like one of themselves, standing there with his children holding his hands,
was after all the right King for England; for there was not
a dissentient voice.

Exactly five months later—on the morning of May
12, 1937—the King and Queen drove to their Coronation at
Westminster Abbey through streets lined by millions of
men, women and children. The traditional route of the procession had been lengthened and carried northward, to give
the poorer citizens a chance to see the splendid cavalcade,
for the Sovereign who had come to the Throne was to earn
his name of "The Working Man's King." Since his accession he had already saved industry hundreds of thousands

of pounds and averted large-scale unemployment by refusing to change the Coronation date fixed by King Edward VIII. Postponement would have spelled ruin for manufacturers all over the country who had been concentrating for the last year on the production of pottery, medals, and every kind of Coronation ware.

Yet the cheers of those millions lining the route were for the pomp and pageantry of a Royal Procession rather than for personal love of the King and Queen passing by in their gold-encrusted State Coach, drawn by eight Windsor grays. The nation had survived the shock of the Abdication, proving to an astonished world the extent of the British capacity for abstract loyalty to the Crown. Yet probably no one realized more than the King himself the prejudice against him. A small minority in the country was carrying out a calculated campaign, which had met with some success. Fantastic rumors had been deliberately spread—the King was said to be an epileptic; Princess Margaret, deaf and dumb. They reached such a pitch that Mr. R. R. Hyde, who as Director of the Industrial Welfare Society had been closely associated with the Duke of York in the past, gave a public denial to "the malicious and cruel gossip regarding the King."

As the King and Queen entered the Abbey to the fanfare of trumpets many of those who knew them best thought that they looked remote, self-dedicated—as though the loneliness of that high destiny had already touched them.

In a blaze of splendor the first Scottish Queen that England had ever known walked to the altar for her anointing. Her face was pale above her ivory satin dress

with its magnificently embroidered train of purple and er-
mine spread out in a great fan behind her, and carried by
six Maids of Honor. For one moment she looked up to the
Royal Gallery, where Queen Mary stood with the little
Princesses beside her—fairy-tale figures in their white lace
dresses, minute trains and gold circlets—then she knelt in
prayer. Her eyes still held that look of dedication when the
Archbishop of Canterbury placed on her head the Queen's
Crown, with the fabulous Koh-i-noor diamond flashing in
the center, and put into her hands the Scepter with the
Dove and the Ivory Rod. Only once, at the end of the ceremony, just before she passed with the King into the Chapel
of Edward the Confessor, a faint smile touched the corner
of her lips. Little Princess Margaret, leaning down from the
Gallery, watching the proceedings with rapt attention, had
dropped a chocolate over the rail.

Chapter 8

HOMEMAKING in a palace is very much the same as anywhere else, except that it is on a bigger scale. The Queen,
who had always had the gift for creating the atmosphere
of home, as a girl at Glamis and as a bride at 145 Piccadilly,
brought the same touch to bear on the gloomy magnificence of Buckingham Palace.

Before the Coronation almost every hour of her time
was given up to audiences, consultations with officials, and
fittings for robes and regalia. She was so exhausted after the
long Coronation ceremony, and the drive to and from the
Abbey, that on returning to Buckingham Palace she lost
her voice for several hours. She could only throw herself
into Alah's arms and whisper, "I'm so glad it's all over."
Later—after her old nurse had put her to bed for a while—
she recovered that radiant vitality which has always been
one of her great assets, and was able to appear on the balcony with the King and the Princesses.

Now, with the excitement of the Coronation over, the
Queen began to organize her household, undaunted by its

magnificence. She laughed when Georgina Guèrin, coming back from France to take charge of the Princesses during the first holidays after the Accession, was overawed by the new status of her employers. "Everything is so different now," the French girl explained. "I feel quite shy with all of you."

The Queen smiled, a little sadly. "Only circumstances change, Georgina. People stay the same."

The cold impersonality of vast salons gleaming with gilt and marble, and heavy with velvet and brocade, was dispelled by familiar possessions brought from 145 Piccadilly—books, cushions, photographs—and by flowers everywhere. The long shadowy corridors wakened to life with the voices of children, the sound of running footsteps and the patter of dogs. A hutchful of rabbits took up residence in the garden; two venerable toads and a turtle were installed in one of the summerhouses. There were children's parties at the Palace that winter; rooms that had not been disturbed for half a century echoed to the laughter of Blind Man's Buff and Musical Chairs. Even the oldest and most sedate members of the Household caught the new atmosphere.

Gradually the King and Queen began to modernize their home. The King had the tennis courts reconditioned and a swimming pool installed. The Queen wrestled with the problem of household equipment, in which the Palace was years behind the times. Electric light had only recently been installed; the bedrooms had vast grates built for old-fashioned coal fires; and the corridors had no heating of any kind. Many of the kitchen appliances and cooking utensils dated from Queen Victoria's youth. The enormous copper pans and cauldrons were later given over to the scrap-iron drive during the war—to the Queen's relief.

In those early years of their residence at the Palace she planned a number of improvements, but before most of them could be carried out, the war intervened, and the Royal Household, like every other in the country, had to grapple with its inconveniences to the best of its ability. Going through the first post-war exhibition of new kitchens organized by the Gas Industry the Queen sighed in unaffected envy of the new cookers and water heaters. "We've got no such luxuries in Buckingham Palace," she said ruefully.

She brought to the new tasks which confronted her as Queen Consort the gaiety and sound common sense which have always balanced the Celtic strain in her character. Like many Scottish women she is practical to her finger tips. In the business world she would have made a first-class executive. Very few people know that she was behind some of the most successful war-relief schemes, or that the famous "Wings for Victory Week," which brought in over six hundred million pounds in savings for the nation, was her idea.

Her organizing ability came to her help in the complete reshaping of her domestic life. Instead of having a compact and comparatively small household to run, she had now to control a vast establishment divided into a series of water-tight compartments, and a staff numbered in hundreds. She did it without sacrificing the personal element. Although the Royal Household included its own hierarchy of house-keepers, stewards and heads of the different departments, the entire domestic side was under the Queen's supervision.

Nothing escaped her. She knew the precise amount of linen that was in use at Buckingham Palace, and how much remained in reserve. She decided what rooms needed redecorating, and chose the material for new curtains and quilts. She kept a notebook with the names of the guests who came to stay, and their particular likes and dislikes, so that their suites could be decorated with their favorite flowers, and their accustomed cereal could appear for breakfast.

She always interviewed the chef every morning, and chose the menus for the day—whether they were for an ordinary family meal or a State banquet. She introduced many of her own recipes, handed down from her mother, into the Palace menus, and gave instructions for making them. When State dinner parties were held she arranged with the Lord Chamberlain—the Head Officer of the Royal Household—the order of seating, and chose all the table decorations. Very often she went into the dining room for a last minute inspection on her way to dress for dinner.

Her daily routine was a strenuous one now. It still began with the early session given over to the children, which had become an institution. Ever since their babyhood the two little girls had come down to their parents' room for a morning romp, and although the original hour had to be halved after the move to Buckingham Palace, the King, who had seen in his own youth the loneliness that so often surrounds a throne, clung to this reminder of their private life. It was often the only time in the day which he could give to his children. The Queen too loved that daily session with her family, although it usually meant overcrowding the rest of the morning.

Much of the day's work was given to dealing with her enormous correspondence. After the mail had been disposed of there were visitors to be received—Ambassadors' wives, Government officials, representatives of women's organizations. Most afternoons were filled by some public function or other; most evenings by receptions. Sittings with photographers and appointments with hairdressers and dressmakers were fitted into odd half-hours.

As Duchess of York she had never concerned herself very much with fashion. When nearly every other woman was wearing a sleek hair-line, combed off the face and tapering into an Eton crop, she kept to the soft waves and straight-cut fringe which suited her better than any other style. She chose the type of clothes in which she looked her best—tweed suits for morning; chiffons and lace for evening in pastel shades which accentuated her clear coloring, and which the Duke liked. He had the Englishman's conservative taste in dress, and a preference for seeing his wife in pale blue. But as Queen, with the eyes of the nation focused on her, a more regal style of dress became an obligation.

It was in July 1938, when she accompanied the King on a State visit to France, that she wore for the first time the beautiful picture dresses for evening which will always be associated with her.

The official program of the visit, which included banquets and receptions, a gala performance at the opera and garden parties and other functions, necessitated a complete trousseau of clothes, but the difficulty was that the Queen was in mourning for her mother, Lady Strathmore, who had died only a few weeks previously. The sight of a Royal visitor heavily draped in black would have cast gloom over

French hospitality, but white has been traditionally per-
missible as Royal mourning, so the Queen and her dress-
maker, Norman Hartnell, devised an all-white wardrobe, extending even to accessories.

The purpose of the visit—to strengthen the bonds of
friendship between Britain and her chief ally in Europe—
was obvious to all who could foresee the coming conflict,
and in spite of subsequent events it was achieved. The
warmth of personal affection kindled among the French
people by this young King and Queen who appealed to their
imagination outlived even the bleak years of the German
Occupation which was to follow so soon afterward. All
classes united to welcome them. Even the little Princesses
at home in England were not forgotten, for two of the most
beautiful and lifelike dolls ever created, complete with
wardrobes made by the greatest Parisian dressmakers, were
sent over as presents to them.

It was especially the Queen's triumph. Her wonderful
crinoline dresses in white lace and tulle, which were actually inspired by the famous Winterhalter portraits of the
young Queen Victoria at Buckingham Palace, caused a sen-
sation. Worn with her magnificent pearls and diamonds the
effect was dramatic at a time when the fashionable line was
straight, skirts were pencil-slim, and almost every woman
wore her hair in a long page-boy bob. The entire French
press raved over the Queen of England's blue eyes, Dresden
china skin and softly waved hair.

Her great charm has always been her coloring. Like
her daughter the young Queen, the Queen Mother is not
photogenic. No photograph has ever done her justice. King
George VI used to tell the story of the American Senator

from Texas who was presented to them both on their visit to Washington. After staring at the Queen for a moment in speechless admiration, he burst out: "Ma'am, you sure are a thousand times prettier than your portraits."

The Canadian tour in the early summer of 1939, which included a three-day visit to the United States, had also a vital bearing on the future. It was perhaps a greater personal triumph for the King and Queen than was generally realized at the time. The people of Canada had been rudely shaken by the Abdication, for the Prince of Wales had been known and loved there as one of themselves ever since he had bought his ranch in the West. The new Sovereigns were strangers to the vast crowds who lined the streets of Quebec to greet them, and much depended on that first impression. But from the moment of their landing a bond of sympathy was established. It was strengthened at every stage of the 6,000-mile tour.

In Quebec, where the King gave pleasure to hundreds of thousands of French-Canadians by replying to the official speeches of welcome in perfect French; in Montreal, where the newspapers came out with banner headlines, "Roi, Reine Ont Reconquis Le Canada"; in Ottawa, where the opening of the Federal Parliament provided a spectacle of splendid pageantry and left an indelible memory of two young Sovereigns—the King in his Field Marshal's uniform, the Queen in a magnificent dress of white satin embroidered in gold—receiving the homage of the Senate. In Glengarry where the descendants of Scottish settlers turned out to the last man, woman, and child to give a Gaelic greeting to Canada's first Scottish-born Queen; in Toronto where hundreds of working girls sacrificed their lunch hour to

strew flowers in the path of the Royal procession; in Winni-
peg where the Queen broadcast a message to the women of
Canada that was relayed throughout the country—it was
the same story all the way. The whole tour from coast to
coast aroused an enthusiasm which the King himself described as "an overwhelming testimony of good will from
young and old alike." The romantic figure of the Prince
of Wales had been quietly superseded by that of a modest
young man whose slow, deliberate speech, somehow carried
conviction and sincerity.

In the United States, too, the King and Queen built
up good will which was to be of the utmost importance in
the war years. Their unaffected enjoyment of the whole-
hearted welcome of the New Yorkers, who showered ticker-
tape on them and yelled themselves hoarse, was a revelation
to millions of ordinary Americans prepared for Royalty to
be poker-faced and unapproachable. The informality with
which they shook hands with everyone who was presented
to them, and went round among the guests at the reception
given for them in Washington by President and Mrs.
Roosevelt won over the press. "We like them, and we hope
they like us," commented one of the newspapers. The time
would come when this liking would take the tangible form
of food parcels and clothing for stricken Britain.

In August of 1939 the Royal Family went up to Balmoral as usual. It had been a wonderful summer of sunshine and bumper harvests everywhere in Europe; the
Scottish moors had never looked lovelier, but by now the
war clouds which had been gathering all through the past
year were black overhead. Already Germany was echoing to
the tramp of marching men and the rumble of guns mov-

ing up to the Polish frontier. Every day there were urgent dispatches from London, or Ministers coming up to Balmoral for consultations. There was no rest for the King. Everyone around him noticed how tired and worn he looked.

The Queen, too, felt the strain of those weeks, although to outward appearances she was still gay and full of fun, going for picnics on the moors with the children and Georgina Guèrin or fishing with Princess Elizabeth. Mother and daughter were beginning to be companions now, for the thirteen-year-old Princess was mature for her age. She was studying seriously, in a wide field of subjects. The Queen, who had continued all through the years to supervise the education of both her daughters, had arranged for her to read Constitutional History with Sir Henry Marten, then Vice-Provost of Eton. Her father discussed politics and world affairs with her as he would with an adult, visualizing a day when this slim little schoolgirl daughter would be called to a Throne.

Life was not altogether too serious for her. The Queen saw to that. She was determined to give her children plenty of time for play. There was no need to worry where Princess Margaret was concerned. She made fun for herself and all those around her. But Princess Elizabeth was sensitive and conscientious—almost too conscientious for her age. And so the Queen called her away from her books, to ride or fish, or even to make a cake for tea. She liked cooking—which she had learned in the first place as a Girl Guide—and on wet days at Balmoral she would often go down to the big old-fashioned kitchen and turn out a batch of scones.

The long-drawn suspense of those August days culminated in the King's hurried return to Buckingham Palace. The Queen remained in the Highlands for another day or two with her daughters until she could bear it no longer; then she too went back to London. "If things turn out badly I must be with the King," she told Georgina Guèrin.

Before leaving Balmoral she called Princess Elizabeth to her and explained that she would now be the temporary head of the family, and must be responsible for the Household. The little girl took the injunction very seriously. Georgina Guèrin still remembers her indignation over the first A.R.P. notices which were put up on the walls of the corridors at Balmoral. When the Princess read that "in the event of fire the King, Queen and Princesses must be evacuated immediately," without a reference to the rest of the Household, her eyes flashed.

"And what about the other people in the Castle?" she exclaimed. "Are they to be just left to burn?"

She would not rest until she had gone into the whole question and discovered that ample provision had in fact been made for evacuating everyone in the building.

Chapter *9*

In the two years and nine months that had passed since those December nights in 1936 when bewildered crowds had waited outside 145 Piccadilly, the King and Queen who had come to the Throne so soberly had won the whole nation's respect. It took the war to make them beloved; to bring them close to every home in the country.

For the first time since the days of chivalry, when kings rode out to lead their armies in person, a Sovereign shared the risks of his fighting men. The enemy planes that bombed Bermondsey and Shoreditch did not spare Buckingham Palace.

In those wartime years, the Queen became identified with every mother and every housewife. Her portrait, hanging on the walls of village institutes all over the country, became the face of a friend; her broadcasts—with their homely references to children evacuated and other problems which all women were up against—carried comfort because she spoke from experience.

The Royal Family knew every discomfort and pinprick

known to the rest of the English in those days. The Queen
wrestled with clothes rationing worries—she herself had a
strictly limited number of coupons to cover her official
wardrobe, but her daughters had only the ordinary allow-
ance, and they grew out of their clothes as fast as any other
mother's children. The Royal Household—like every other
—had to get used to Spam, dried eggs and corned beef;
shiver in baths containing only five inches of hot water; and
wait weeks on end for the return of clean linen from the
laundry.

At the start of the Battle of Britain the Queen was
urged to go to Canada with her children for the duration of
the war, but she refused even to consider the idea. She herself would not leave the King, and both he and she felt
that it would be unfair to give their own daughters special
privileges and remove them from risks to which thousands
of other British children were exposed. The Princesses had
a propaganda value too—Lord Haw-Haw several times announced as proof of the imminent collapse of Britain that
they had been sent overseas. Their presence was a sign of
confidence in ultimate victory. So they were evacuated to
Windsor Castle, away from the London raids, but the King
and Queen had still to worry over them, as other parents
were worrying; and not without cause. Windsor was raided
several times. The Princesses spent nights in the shelters
at the Castle, and took cover from flying bombs in the day-
time raids where they could—as thousands of other children were doing. Every evening the Queen telephoned to
them from blitzed London and was comforted by their
happy voices, talking of ordinary things.

She herself remained with the King at Buckingham

Palace all through the London raids, except for rare week ends when they could spare the time to join their children at Windsor. Both of them went about London, disregarding warnings, visiting the worst blitzed areas almost before the smoke of the bombs had cleared. There was little they could do, but their presence brought comfort and a sense of fellow-feeling to families who had lost everything.

"I'm glad we've been bombed too," the Queen said to one of her friends after Buckingham Palace had received a direct hit. "It makes me feel I can look those East End mothers in the face."

In actual fact the Palace was bombed nine times, and one bomb fell less than forty yards from the room in which the King and Queen were sitting.

Down in the much-bombed areas of dockland they still talk of the Queen's kindness after raids—not only of her gifts of clothing and furniture, but of little practical acts of sympathy. An air raid warden told me that he remembered her visiting one street that was little more than a mass of rubble. In one of the few still remaining houses an old woman was in great distress because her dog—a little terrier—had been so frightened by the bomb that it had taken refuge in a hole under the staircase and refused to come out, even for food or water.

"Perhaps I can coax him out for you," said the Queen, who has had an instinct for handling dogs all her life. She knelt down in front of the hole and in a few minutes the terrier was restored to its owner.

In another house a mother whose arm had been injured by falling debris was trying unsuccessfully to dress her baby when the Queen called.

"Give him to me," the Queen said. Without waiting
for an answer she finished dressing the baby, with practiced
hands.

To the Americans her cheerful courage in those darkest
days of the war became symbolic of the spirit of British
women. Millions of people throughout the States handed
round leaflets carrying her picture with the verse composed
in her honor by a Chicago woman:

TRIBUTE TO A QUEEN

London Bridge is falling down,
  My fair Lady!
Be it said to your renown
That you wore your gayest gown,
Your bravest smile, and stayed in Town
When London Bridge was falling down,
  My fair Lady!

It won innumerable friends for Britain, at a time when
"Keep-out-of-the-war" feeling was running high.

The Queen's wartime day often stretched to sixteen or
seventeen hours. At eight o'clock every morning she was at
her desk dealing with her correspondence. She was never in
bed before midnight. The hours between were filled by
conferences with the heads of the women's services; visits
to hospitals and First Aid Posts; tours of anti-aircraft bat-
teries and lonely searchlight units. Without becoming
identified with any particular organization, she gave a lead
to all women's wartime activities.

Very often her own intuition supplied the personal, essentially feminine, touch in a difficult situation. On hearing

that children who had been evacuated were pouring back into the danger zones because of friction with foster parents, she had the idea of sending out a letter of thanks adorned with her own Coat of Arms, to over three hundred thousand homes which had taken in evacuees. It caused immense pleasure. All over the country doors which had been on the point of closing against the strangers were thrown open again.

It was the Queen, too, who suggested, in that dreary October of 1940, when the land was full of anxious parents and homesick children, that the fourteen-year-old Princess Elizabeth should broadcast to children all over the Empire, and especially to those separated from their homes. Mother and daughter worked together on the script, which had a touching sincerity. Millions of people were cheered by the ring of confidence in the young voice.

> I can truthfully say that we children at home are full of cheerfulness and courage. We are trying to do all we can to help our gallant sailors, soldiers, and airmen; and we are trying too to bear our own share of the danger and sadness of war. We know, everyone of us, that in the end all will be well.

And most listeners will remember the impromptu ending when Princess Elizabeth—hating to leave her little sister out of anything—suddenly called, "Come on, Margaret," and a small rather breathless voice piped in, in perfect imitation of a Children's Hour compère, "Good night children, everywhere."

Daily life in those war years was as much disorganized for the Queen as for everyone else. Instead of the orderly program of the past, with every engagement entered in her diary for weeks ahead, she had to plan her day almost from hour to hour. At one moment she would be immersed in affairs of State—acting as a Counsellor of State when the King was overseas, holding an Investiture at Buckingham Palace in his place. At another she would be just a harassed British housewife, trying to reconcile her family to rabbit as a substitute for chicken, thinking out disguises for corned beef, and coping with all the other domestic problems of a Royal Household depleted by the war of two-thirds of its staff. The only respite either for her or for the King in those days was a week end at Windsor, when that was possible. Walking in the grounds with their daughters, followed by the dogs, they could forget for a while the cares of a kingdom at war in the familiar atmosphere of home.

The war years passed over this very British family, bringing them the experiences of so many others. They knew personal sorrow when the Duke of Kent was killed on active service in the aircraft crash in the late summer of 1942. The King grieved for the light-hearted, impulsive younger brother, who had been associated in the past far more closely with the Prince of Wales than with himself, but who had proved so loyal a friend since his Accession.

The Queen knew the anxiety of thousands of wives when the King was overseas, visiting his Armies in the field; his Fleets at sea; his Air Force in the Libyan desert. She had too the experience of so many mothers of seeing her children grow up almost in a flash, in the forcing-house of war. At one moment Princess Elizabeth was a long-legged schoolgirl, racing Margaret in the Park at Windsor; at the next she was a smart young officer in the A.T.S., inclined to patronize her family, and causing consternation to elderly statesmen by driving alone through the London traffic.

And at last came that evening of May 8, 1945, when the King and Queen stood with their daughters on the balcony of Buckingham Palace, watching a crowd that surged round the gates like a sea, cheering frenziedly because the war was over. But now the cheers were no longer those of abstract loyalty. They had the warmth of personal friendliness for a family that had lived and suffered and conquered with all the rest.

Chapter *10*

THE war left its imprint on the Royal Family as on every other in Britain.

The King and Queen who had worked untiringly through the long years of suspense felt, like millions of their subjects, the inevitable reaction when the tension was relaxed. Yet there could be no let up for them as for those others. The King was immersed in postwar problems—a change of government at home, after a bitterly contested General Election; the resettlement of Europe; conflicting political interests in the Dominions. The Queen was faced with the reconstruction of her public life; with the resumption of entertaining and of many social activities which had been in abeyance for the last six years; with the reorganization of a Household dispersed by the war. She was also pre-occupied as a mother just then, mainly on account of Princess Elizabeth.

One of the closest friends of the Royal Family once said to me, "Isn't there a saying that being a good mother depends mostly on just being someone to whom your children always go? It describes the Queen Mother perfectly. All through their lives her daughters have taken all their joys and sorrows and problems to her."

This was never more true than of the time when Princess Elizabeth was making her first shy acquaintance with love. Very few people, even today, know how much she owed to her mother's understanding sympathy.

Like so many girls of her generation the Princess had no formal coming-out. She simply began to be seen at more dinner parties at Buckingham Palace—very grown up in her first evening dress of white satin embroidered in gold—and to take on more public duties. She had her own little suite at the Palace; a bedroom, bathroom and sitting room. She chose the decorations and chintzes, and put out all her photographs and books with great pride.

At nineteen she was completely unaffected and devoid of the shyness that afflicted so many of Queen Victoria's descendants. She talked easily and happily to everyone, from Winston Churchill—who was a frequent guest both at Windsor Castle and Buckingham Palace—to the evacuees from Whitechapel who joined her Girl Guide company. Probably no Heir to the Throne of England has ever had so democratic an upbringing.

People all over the country were surprised to read in their newspapers on the morning of August 16, 1945, the story of how the Princesses had gone out of Buckingham Palace the night before, accompanied only by two young Guards officers, and joined the vast crowds celebrating the final victory over Japan. But no one who knew the Royal Family intimately wondered at it, for it was precisely the sort of thing the King and Queen would encourage their daughters to do.

All through the war years the Princesses mixed with people of all types. They went hiking with their company of Girl Guides and camped out with them in the grounds of Windsor Castle—not with a few handpicked children, daughters of Court officials, but with the rank and file of evacuees from the East End. They did their share of the washing-up and potato-peeling—in fact Princess Elizabeth did considerably more, for she was so unselfish that the rest were inclined to impose on her. They slept in sleeping bags in a tent, and got up earlier than the others when it was their turn to fry the sausages for breakfast. The Queen, who had been keen on the Girl Guide movement in her own girlhood, and had been District Commissioner for the Glamis Association, wanted her daughters to have this experience.

The deft way in which they handled their domestic chores was sometimes a revelation to the other girls in the company. The truth was that both of them had been initiated in housework through looking after Princess Elizabeth's "Little House," for the Queen had made a condition that they should keep it in order themselves, without any help from the servants at Royal Lodge. They cleaned the different rooms once a week, and gave the whole house a thorough spring cleaning every year—taking out all the carpets and shampooing them, and washing all the paint. As a result both of them today know far more about the practical running of an ordinary house than many middle-class girls.

One of Princess Margaret's friends—a young married

woman who has recently moved into a London flat—told me that she had been worried over a deep stain on the bath-tub, left by the previous tenants, which had defied all efforts. She happened to mention it to Princess Margaret, who said at once, "Oh, I know how you can get it off." The treatment she suggested was the right one. The stain completely disappeared.

Everyone heard in those war years of how the Princesses were taking leading parts in Christmas pantomimes produced at Windsor Castle in aid of the Queen's Wool Fund, but only a few people knew that the whole idea originated with the Queen. Wanting to give her daughters something to do which would both provide an interest in dreary wartime days, and make them feel that they were helping the national effort, she remembered the pleasure which she had had as a child from private theatricals at Glamis. She suggested to Mr. Hubert Tanner, the headmaster of the Royal School at Windsor, that he should get up an entertainment in which the Princesses could take part with his pupils and the evacuee children from London. It was so successful that it became a Christmas institution all through the war, and the productions grew more ambitious every year. Both the Princesses had a distinct talent for acting, Princess Margaret especially, and the experience which they gained in appearing before an audience and overcoming stage fright in their childhood has been a great asset to them in public life.

From their earliest years the Queen Mother shaped the training of both her daughters to give them independence of outlook, humanity, and poise. They were taught all the little social graces before they were out of the nursery—

Alah was a rigid disciplinarian where good manners were concerned. Princess Elizabeth began practicing the art of entertaining on her cousins, Princess Mary's two little boys, and on Lord and Lady Allendale's children—the next-door neighbors at 145 Piccadilly. Later, in the war years, her mother encouraged her to give informal tea parties for the young officers stationed at Windsor Castle. Many of them still remember the homey picture of the tea table drawn up in front of a blazing log fire on winter afternoons, and Princess Elizabeth sitting behind the teapot, while Princess Margaret plied them with cakes and sandwiches. A very old friend of the Bowes-Lyon family, who happened to drop in for one of these parties, told me that he was struck by the resemblance of Princess Elizabeth to her mother as he had known her in the days of the First World War. She had even in her teens the same graciousness and the same gift for making everyone feel at ease in her presence.

All these contacts with the outer world broke down the barrier which has traditionally surrounded Royalty. The Princess Elizabeth who registered at the local Labor Exchange at Windsor on her sixteenth birthday, April 21, 1942, was very much like any other normal, self-reliant, uninhibited girl in the country. But when she reached calling-up age two years later, and begged to be allowed to joint one of the women's Services, she met with opposition —for the first time in her life—from her father. She was after all Heir to the Throne, eligible to serve as a Counsellor of State when the King was abroad. Besides receiving specialized education and training she was already carrying out a number of public duties. He had decided that this apprenticeship in ruling must not be interrupted by war service, and at first he was adamant in his refusal.

It was the Queen who turned the scales in her daughter's favor. Realizing that Lilibet's heart was set on playing her part in the war, not as the future Queen of England but like any other girl of her own generation, she persuaded the King to change his mind. So the Princess got her way and joined the A.T.S. as a subaltern, and the King was very proud of his daughter in her trim khaki uniform when he drove down to Aldershot with the Queen and Princess Margaret to visit her training center. It pleased him that she insisted on going through the full course in mechanics, and on being treated like everyone else in the mess, taking her turn as duty officer with the rest, saluting her seniors, and learning to drive and service all types of vehicle—from staff cars to heavy trucks and field ambulances. She has a flair for engineering and is as good a mechanic as Prince Philip, although when they go anywhere by car she usually leaves the driving to him.

In that year of 1945 when peace came at last to a battered Europe, Princess Elizabeth was a lovely girl with the Dresden china coloring of her mother's family and Queen Mary's light blue eyes. And by now she was in love.

Prince Philip—that flaxen-haired little boy whom she had met for the first time at a children's party when he was ten and she was five—had come back into her life just before the war.

In the summer of 1939 King George VI paid a visit to the Royal Naval College at Dartmouth and took the Queen and the two Princesses with him. The Commanding Officer of the College entertained them to tea, and suggested that they might like one of his cadets to join the party.

The guest was a tall good-looking boy, only one among nine hundred other cadets, and of minor importance as it was his first term, but as Prince Philip of Greece he was a distant relative of the Royal Family. At tea he sat next to the thirteen-year-old Princess Elizabeth, but their meeting was no more memorable than their previous one in the Mountbatten nursery. She was shy and blushed like a peony every time he spoke to her; he was more interested in the sandwiches and cream cakes. But he showed her round the College.

"I will say she seems brighter than most girls," he said reflectively to one of the cadets afterward. "She asked a lot of quite intelligent questions."

Gordonstoun was only a few months behind him in that summer of 1939. Getting into Dartmouth had represented the first big hurdle in his life. In spite of his connections with the Royal Family—and the Navy has its own hierarchy and is apt to be unimpressed by princes—he was still a foreigner in Britain and he was sufficiently aware of the international situation to realize its probable effect on his own life.

Letters from his sisters and their German husbands were growing more and more despondent. A career in the British Navy would mean separation from them, but he had already made his decision.

He was too old when he left Gordonstoun to enter Dartmouth in the normal way. His only chance was through open competition, in the special entry examination. Although he was the right type for the Navy—intelligent, athletic, uninhibited and a good mixer—he was academically only average.

The exam was a stiff one, and he was weak in some of the essential subjects. Nobody at Gordonstoun would have been surprised if he had failed—but for the fact that he was determined to pass into Dartmouth at all costs, and with him his own determination is always the deciding factor.

He worked in his last year at school as one inspired, passed the exam somewhere about the middle of the list of thirty-odd entrants, and entered Dartmouth in May of 1939. At the same time he applied for British citizenship, but the application was destined to be held up—with thousands of others—by the outbreak of war.

Gordonstoun was a useful preparation for Dartmouth. A boy who had sailed cutters off the Moray coast off and on for the past four years, been a member of a schooner's crew on two cruises, and learned from coastguards how to handle rocket and breeches buoy equipment made a good candidate for the Navy—so good in fact that Prince Philip was awarded the King's Dirk as the best cadet of his term, and another prize as the best cadet of the year.

He was only in his second term when the war broke out, but boys grew up quickly in those wartime years. In January, 1940, he went to sea, just one midshipman more in the British Navy, but with the difference that he was serving a country that was not his own.

The war had cut him off completely from his family. His father was still in France, where he died in 1944. His mother was in Greece, working for the Red Cross.

The husbands of three of his sisters were already with the German armed forces.

His first posting was to the battleship *Ramillies* in which he served with suitable humility as the youngest of the midshipmen. A year later he was mentioned in dispatches for courage and efficiency when in charge of a section of his ship's searchlight control during the night battle of Cape Matapan in which the Italian Fleet was routed.

After that his career was meteoric, as many naval careers were during the war. By January, 1942, he was a sub-lieutenant appointed to H.M.S. *Wallace,* a destroyer engaged on convoy escort duty in the North Sea. By the following July he was lieutenant, and three months later first lieutenant of the ship, the youngest officer—at twenty-one—ever to hold the post in a destroyer of that size.

He was perhaps more lonely in those first years of the war than ever before or since. He had always been accustomed to spend at least a part of his school holidays with one or another of his sisters, for they had been a united family, but now that was impossible.

The Queen, with motherly kindness, thought that he might sometimes feel his loneliness when he came home on leave, so, although there was no idea of him in those days as a possible husband for her daughter, she asked him once of twice to informal dinners at Buckingham Palace, followed by the theatre. He did not see Princess Elizabeth, who had been evacuated to Windsor Castle with Princess Margaret, and was still having schoolgirl suppers in front of the nursery fire there. But he heard a lot of her for the Queen, like every mother, loved to talk about her children. He was shown snapshots, and letters, and programs of the pantomimes at Windsor, and naturally the next step was to ask him down to see one.

He sat with the King and Queen in the front row, roared with laughter at all the jokes, and applauded vigorously at the end of the performance. But the memory he carried back to his ship was of a new Princess Elizabeth, a seventeen-year-old girl, very demure and self-possessed in her role of an Edwardian beauty, and very lovely in her dress of rose tulle embroidered with turquoise.

For the rest of the week end at Windsor they saw a lot of each other, played games in the corridors with Princess Margaret, and romped with the corgis in the Great Park. It would be absurd to say that they fell in love, or even that they realized that they were attracted to each other in those early days but from that time they began to correspond, and as the months passed Prince Philip like thousands of other young men overseas found that a girl's letters grew to mean more and more to him.

Princess Elizabeth, even in those days, wrote charmingly. Both she and Princess Margaret formed the habit of expressing themselves easily and naturally on paper in their childhood, when their mother used to give each of them a diary on New Year's Day, and insist on their writing it up every evening before they went to bed. So in the long weeks at sea her letters, with their vivid pictures of home, were to Prince Philip all that a pen-friend's letters were to many a man in the Services. And perhaps before he even realized it himself he fell in love with her.

It was probably the Queen who noticed first that this adolescent friendship had changed to love. She certainly knew in that autumn of 1945 that her nineteen-year-old daughter had had a photograph of Prince Philip on her mantelpiece for some time. Still Princess Elizabeth seemed

such a child when they went up to Balmoral for the first
carefree holiday since the war. Hearing her untroubled
laugh as she set out with the keepers for a day's deer-
stalking, or for a ride with Princess Margaret, her mother
could not believe that the shaft of love had gone very deep.

There was only one cloud to shadow the Queen's happiness in that first year after the war, when Alah died, very
suddenly. The whole family grieved for her, for although
the Princesses had long outgrown the nursery, Alah had
been a fixture in the household. No one had even imagined
a time when she would not be there, with her knitting and
her stories of the past. The Queen loved to run up to the
old nursery for a cosy chat with her. She had clung to that
link with her childhood even more since she had lost her
father, Lord Strathmore, during the war. All through the
years Alah had shared every joy, given comfort in every
sorrow, stood by in every ordeal, calm and unruffled. She
had smoothed the Coronation robes of the Queen with a
loving hand before she drove to Westminster and whispered encouragingly, "Now, don't worry, dear. You'll see
it will all go off beautifully," just as she had done when
the little Elizabeth Bowes-Lyon went to her first party.

Her death was a great blow to the Queen. "I feel that
so much of my own life has gone with Alah," she told one
of her friends.

As the year 1946 wore on all those who knew them
intimately realized that Princess Elizabeth and Prince
Philip were deeply in love. The Prince was stationed at
Corsham in Wiltshire now, training petty officers, but he
often came up to Buckingham Palace, covering the one
hundred miles' distance in his little M.G. car in so short a

Wide World

The Queen smiles at a humorous remark of President Franklin
D. Roosevelt on her arrival in Washington, D.C., during her
first visit to America in 1939.

145

Wide World

The King and Queen with President and Mrs. Franklin D.
Roosevelt and the President's mother on the porch at Hyde
Park.

The King and Queen inspect a rescue squad on a wartime
visit to the Yorkshire coal mining area.

Wide World

British Information Service

The Queen chats with Warden T. Andrews and his wife and baby outside the ruins of their bombed house in Plymouth.

Wide World

The Queen steps lightly over the debris left by a bombing of
Buckingham Palace.

International

Britain's Royal Family at the reunion marking Queen Elizabeth II's coming of age. (*Seated:* Dowager Queen Mary, King George VI, Princess Elizabeth, Queen Elizabeth. *Standing:* the Duke of Gloucester, the Duchess of Gloucester, Princess Margaret, the Princess Royal (Lady Harewood), the Duchess of Kent, Lord Harewood.)

Their Majesties of England attend the ballet at Covent Garden.

European

Wide World

Queen Elizabeth chats with Gen. Charles de Gaulle (*left*) and Vice-Admiral Emile Muselier (*right*), Chief of the Free French Navy, on a visit to the Hospital for Free French Naval Forces near London.

Wide World

King George VI and Queen Elizabeth talk with Cornelius
Mostert, seven-foot-three-inch Swaziland farmer, on their
South African tour in 1947.

Wide World

Four thousand Swazi warriors greet the Royal visitors at
Goedgegun, Africa.

The wedding of Queen Elizabeth II and the Duke of Edinburgh in Westminster Abbey.

International

British Information Services

The Royal grandparents with Prince Charles and Princess
Anne.

Queen Elizabeth in the White Drawing Room of Buckingham Palace.

Wide World

Queen Elizabeth on her fiftieth birthday.

British Information Services

British Information Services

Princess Margaret leaving Buckingham Palace with Queen
Elizabeth on her way to the Trooping of the Color Ceremony.

Wide World

The Queen Mother attends a reception at Grove House,
London.

time that the Queen, always rather a nervous motorist, was quite anxious about him.

"Darling, he mustn't kill himself coming to see you," she would say to Princess Elizabeth.

By now the whole press was beginning to speculate on the romance. The black M.G. with its dark green upholstery, driven by a blond young man, often in blazer and flannels on a hot day, was too different from the more sedate traffic usually associated with Buckingham Palace to escape notice. Every time it was detected driving up to the private entrance a fresh crop of rumors arose. They were distressing to the twenty-year-old Princess and embarrassing to Prince Philip.

He was very much in love and as far as ancestry was concerned he was a match for the daughter of any ruling house in Europe. The Royal Family of Denmark, from which he was descended on his father's side, was one of the greatest in history. His mother's family, the Mountbattens, was closely related to the Sovereigns of England. But in possessions he had little to offer. The insecurity of his childhood, when he had lived with his parents in exile at St. Cloud, had made a deep impression on him.

If Princess Elizabeth had been anyone other than the Heiress to the Throne he would probably have proposed to her sooner than he actually did. The mere fact that even if she loved him they could not get engaged without the formal consent of the King and the approval of Parliament must have brought home to him the difficulties he would have to face as her husband. To every man in love the prospect of marriage must represent the sacrifice of a certain amount of personal freedom. In Prince Philip's case it would mean infinitely more—the subjugation of much of his own personality.

He would have to accept the perpetual glare of publicity, which he loathed, a life of protocol and conventions utterly alien to him, and an increasing burden of responsibilities which would probably spell the end of his career at sea. The identity of Lieutenant Mountbatten, R.N., who had found complete fulfilment in the life of a naval officer with an income in the neighborhood of £8 a week, would have to be submerged in that of the King of England's son-in-law.

The advantages would be immense, of course, but not of the type to weigh very much with a man who had no liking for public life and no urge for self-advancement, except in his own profession. It was a very real conflict in which love ultimately triumphed.

In the meantime a photograph of Prince Philip continued to occupy the place of honor on Princess Elizabeth's dressing table, and when he returned to England, after the Japanese surrender in September, 1945, everyone noticed the change in her personality.

She began to wear more sophisticated clothes, and to choose them herself. Until then she had had no interest in fashion—unlike Princess Margaret—and had been guided by the Queen's taste. Now for the first time she looked critically at herself. She altered her hair style to a simpler, sleeker one that was much more becoming to her; she used powder and lipstick, sparingly but with growing confidence, and a touch of perfume in the evenings. There was a new depth in her smile. Her whole personality had the sparkle of a girl in love.

In the meantime the King and Queen were growing attached to this forthright and uninhibited young man who crashed into the Palace setting of gilt and red plush with a disregard of ceremony that delighted them as much as it shocked some members of their entourage. No one had ever thought of walking about Buckingham Palace in a blazer, still less in gray flannel trousers and a tennis shirt, until Prince Philip did it, with a sublime unconsciousness of the precedent he was creating.

The summer of 1946, when he spent his leave at Balmoral as a guest of the King and Queen, was the deciding factor in Prince Philip's love for Princess Elizabeth. In the formality of Buckingham Palace, always surrounded by other people, neither of them had been sure of their feelings. They had gone to the theatre together and found that they shared the same tastes in plays, danced together and found that their steps matched perfectly, and discovered a mutual liking for a great many things. But by that time their interest in one another had become public property.

Every time they appeared anywhere together, even in the same theatre party, the rumors broke out afresh. The whole nation seemed to have a part in the affair. The little M.G. was recognized driving into Buckingham Palace and warmly cheered by the spectators. Princess Elizabeth, visiting a factory, was greeted on her arrival with cries of "Where's Philip?"

One of the few houses where they could meet in those days without publicity was Coppins. The Duchess of Kent, who had been up against the same problem before her own marriage, often invited them down together for a tennis party or an informal dance. Queen Mary, too, who was strongly in favor of the marriage from the first, used to ask them to tea at Marlborough House—by sheer coincidence on the same day. But, even so, the rumors grew until they were caught up by the press of half the world.

But at Balmoral, where they could wander over the lonely moors together, or drive off into the hills for a picnic, they were in a world of their own, and it did not take them long to discover that their love was for a lifetime.

But the King, when Prince Philip asked his permission to propose to the Princess, told him to wait, not—as so many people imagined at the time—because he had any objection to the marriage, but because Princess Elizabeth was a dearly loved daughter, and both her parents wanted to be quite sure that she knew her own mind.

The press had only one interpretation of the delay in the announcement of the engagement—that the King feared Prince Philip might not be acceptable to the nation as a husband for Princess Elizabeth. It was a wrong one. For considerations of State the marriage was suitable in every way. The Prince had all the qualities demanded in a Prince Consort. Where the King and Queen's own views were concerned, the fact that he was making his way in the world as a commoner, and had already a fine record in the Navy, was in his favor. The King, who had been proud when he was presented during the war with the T.U.C. badge and told one of his brothers-in-law that he considered it one of the greatest compliments he had ever received, was sincere in his democracy. The truth was that both he and the Queen were thinking simply like any other parents—of their daughter's happiness. She was only twenty, and they wanted to be quite sure that she was marrying the right man before giving their consent to a formal engagement—for by centuries-old tradition, a Royal engagement must never be broken.

So although Prince Philip spent many happy hours rambling over the moors with the Princess, he was asked to defer his formal request for her hand until the following year. The King and Queen were to start on a tour of South Africa early in 1947, and the Princesses were to accompany them. Princess Elizabeth would be twenty-one when she returned to England and she could make her decision then. The few months' absence would be a test of love, said the King.

It was a wistful Princess Elizabeth who chose her clothes for the South African tour, and sailed with her parents and younger sister on the *Vanguard* on February 1, 1947. Perhaps the Queen, noticing how much thinner her daughter had grown in the last few weeks, worried over her and wondered whether everyone had been too hard on the lovers. Princess Elizabeth had always been so submissive, and she had had so little time for pleasure lately. Ever since her eighteenth birthday she had been caught up in a continuous round of public duties—as her father had been in the days when the young Elizabeth Bowes-Lyon had brought gaiety into his life. The Queen wanted her daughter to find the happiness she herself had found in marriage. And the Duke of York had waited three years for his bride!

Chapter *11*

THE South African tour was a greater personal triumph for the King and Queen than any they had yet known. They traveled through a country torn with political differences; among a people divided by fundamental racial problems, and including minorities opposed even to the principle of Monarchy. To penetrate as Sovereigns into the heart of this territory of conflicting opinions, to meet men and women of many races and of widely diverse views, and to leave behind a healing influence and renewed good will was a major task in kingcraft, but King George VI and his Queen, who had surmounted so many difficulties, were equal to it. Wherever they went—among people black, white, or Indian—they sowed the seeds of friendship for Britain.

The people of Cape Town like to remember that before the Royal Family even landed on South African soil, the Queen set the pattern of friendly informality which was to prevail throughout the tour. On the morning of February 17, as thousands of eyes were straining out anxiously toward the battleship *Vanguard* cutting majestically through the gleaming waters of Table Bay, four solitary figures appeared on the platform high above the guns of the forward turret— the King and Queen and their daughters.

On shore a Royal reception had been prepared for them, with bands and a guard of honor. The Cabinet Ministers, headed by General Smuts, were already beginning to assemble on the red-carpeted dais; a distinguished gathering of civic dignitaries and their wives waited to be presented. The stands erected at the dock were packed with spectators; thousands of school children were massed on the slopes of Signal Hill to form with their white-clad bodies a living slogan—WELCOME.

Suddenly the inevitable sense of tension preceding a Royal visit was broken. One of the four distant figures on the *Vanguard* was seen to be waving gaily. The Queen was greeting those on shore. Immediately a cheer rang out from the vast crowd. That impulsive friendly wave had already established the bond between the Crown and the people of South Africa.

This little incident was typical of the entire tour. Despite the elaborate arrangements made many months ahead, it was evident from the very beginning that the King and Queen put less emphasis on the ceremonial proceedings than on the personal contact with their subjects. They charmed the South Africans, as they had charmed the Australians and Canadians years before, by their warm humanity, by their obvious sincerity, and by the way in which they insisted on cutting short official routine to give them more time for meeting people whose names had not been included in the list of presentations. Again and

again their train—the famous White Train—was delayed
beyond schedule at some stopping place because of Their
Majesties' obstinate refusal to pass by some humble group
hovering at the back of the platform.

This was especially true of the Queen. Realizing that
each day of the 10,000 mile tour with its crowded program of receptions by local councils, formal addresses, and
presentations of leading townspeople, represented an un-
forgettable experience in thousands of simple lives, she was
tireless in her desire to give as much pleasure as possible.
Members of the Royal Household, who traveled on the
White Train with her, remember that no matter how
fatigued she might be she would make a point of sitting by
the window on long runs through sparsely populated country, so that she could wave to some isolated farmer who had
perhaps ridden fifty miles or more on the chance of getting a fleeting glimpse of his Sovereign as the train slowed
down.

Her vivid interest in everyone she met enabled her to
leave each individual man or woman presented to her with
the feeling that he or she had made a personal friend of
the Queen. She attended countless tea parties, rewarded
the wives of officials who had spent days beforehand in
anxious preparation by her frank appreciation of their
cakes, and came away with the recipes to add to her own
collection. She listened to the singing of a choir of Bantu
students and found such genuine pleasure in the beauty of
their songs that, taking the Princesses with her, she spent
more than half an hour going round the ranks of singers
and talking to them.

In a young and ardent country where family ties are

strong the homely appeal of a Royal couple so evidently happy in their marriage was invincible. It was heightened by the presence of their daughters. The crowds everywhere were delighted with the informality of the Princesses who talked to anyone who happened to be nearest when the White Train stopped at wayside stations, and got out on to the platform to pose for amateur photographers.

In Basutoland they gave immense pleasure to seventy thousand Basutos assembled from far and near by reviewing the native Girl Guides, and going across the parade ground afterward to talk to twenty girls who had attended the review in a closed omnibus because they were lepers.

At the little town of Camper, where the Royal train made a short halt, an old man pushed his way through the crowds on the platform to ask Princess Elizabeth to turn her head so that his invalid son, who was lying in a car at the back of the station, could see her. Immediately the Queen heard the request she had the barriers lowered, and took both Princesses over to the car to talk to the boy.

The Queen's effortless charm won over dour old Boers who had been fighting for Kruger at the time when she was a child playing in her nursery.

"I'm very pleased to have met you, Ma'am," one of them told her bluntly, "but we still feel sometimes that we can't forgive the English for having conquered us."

"Oh, I understand that perfectly," she answered. "We feel very much the same in Scotland too."

The entire tour, with its long successions of public functions—ranging from the Opening of Parliament in Salisbury, with much of the traditional ceremonial of Westminster, to the reception in Bechuanaland of native chiefs resplendent in uniforms of their own devising—was in the words of General Smuts "a sustained triumphal progress." For the people of South Africa this first personal contact with their Sovereign made history. But the memories which will be most cherished in countless homes throughout the Dominion, and passed down to future generations will, I think, be of the Queen's kindliness and sympathy. There are any number of instances of her graciousness and tact.

In a mining district of the East Rand where the Royal Party left the train and drove in their car along roads lined by thousands of native miners, she showed her quick wit in an emergency. As the Royal car advanced at walking pace, an enormous Zulu broke out from the crowd and rushed forward, shouting and waving his arms in an apparently threatening way. Still smiling in acknowledgment of the cheers the Queen deftly held him off with the point of her umbrella until police came—and discovered that the only thing he was holding in his hand was a crumpled ten-shilling note which he wanted to present to Princess Elizabeth.

I like, too, the little human incident that happened when they were climbing the granite slopes of the Matopos to the grave of Cecil Rhodes. Halfway up the Queen found that she could not walk another step in her high-heeled cut-away shoes, and Princess Elizabeth had to come to the rescue by lending her mother her own solid pair, and finishing the climb in her stockinged feet.

"It was so like Mummy to set out in those shoes," the Princess told one of her friends afterward. Both the King and his daughters always teased the Queen over her shoes. She has tiny feet—size 2—with very arched insteps and hates wearing, except for country walks, the type of shoes that are called sensible.

The tour of South Africa, successful as it was, was intensely fatiguing, for the program was so closely planned that it scarcely left breathing space between engagements. The whole Royal Family were tired out when they returned to England. The King had lost over fourteen pounds; the Queen was exhausted. Only Princess Elizabeth looked radiant when the *Vanguard* docked at Portsmouth on May 11, 1947.

And now the press comments on the Royal romance broke out with renewed zest. For months there had been nothing to feed the flame of rumor except an announcement in the *London Gazette* in February that Prince Philip had renounced all his foreign titles and taken British nationality. He was now simply Lieutenant Mountbatten. Everyone waited for further news, but there was none. Princess Elizabeth and Prince Philip had not been seen together in public after the Royal Family's return. People began to say that the affair was going to come to nothing. The Prince was not even among the guests of the King and Queen at Windsor Castle for Ascot week.

Only those who were closest to the Royal Family knew that on the last day of the races the Queen gave a dance in the Red Drawing Room at the Castle for one hundred young people, all intimate friends of the Princesses. Lieutenant Philip Mountbatten was there, and he and Princess Elizabeth danced nearly every dance together. A few weeks later the engagement was announced.

Their marriage, on November 20, 1947, has already

passed into history, but it is not generally known that there was some discussion as to where the wedding should take place. Some of the King's advisers were in favor of a quiet, semi-private ceremony at St. George's Chapel, Windsor, with no suggestion of Royal pomp at a time of austerity. But the nation as a whole, weary of the sacrifices of the long war years, was craving for glamour. The final decision lay with Princess Elizabeth and she chose Westminster Abbey—where nearly a quarter of a century before the Lady Elizabeth Bowes-Lyon had plighted her troth to the Duke of York.

"I had a feeling I wanted to be married in the same church as Papa and Mummy," the Princess told one of her friends. "I would like to think that Philip and I were beginning just as they did."

Old friends of the Queen thought she had never looked more charming than on her daughter's wedding day, when she took her place in the Sacrarium of the Abbey, in a dress of apricot brocade which set off her magnificent jewels. No one would have guessed that she had worked—like any other bride's mother—until almost the last day, arranging all the details of the wedding. She had drawn up the lists of invitations and planned the seating of the guests with the Lord Chamberlain's office. She had chosen the menu for the lunch at Buckingham Palace. She had helped her daughter to get her trousseau together, and parted with some of her own clothing coupons to buy material.

The Princess had to be as resourceful as any other bride, and she took away on her honeymoon most of her last year's dresses and several pairs of her mother's stockings. At the Queen's suggestion, Norman Hartnell was asked to curb his imagination and submit sketches for practical clothes needing the minimum of material and simple enough to be worn by any girl. So the Princess' tight-waisted going-away coat—the first fitted coat to be worn for years—swept the country. Thousands of women copied it.

And now all the preparations were complete. Inside Westminster Abbey, resplendent once again in the scarlet and gold of pre-war days, six kings and seven queens—almost all Europe's remaining sovereigns—were assembled among three thousand distinguished guests. Outside was a vast crowd of people, the majority of whom had waited all night. Many were young men and women still in the Forces, or recently demobilized; for this wedding, in spite of its Royal pageantry, had become identified with thousands of other Service weddings. The bridegroom was in the Navy; the bride had served in the A.T.S.; and theirs had been a wartime romance, with all the attendant separation and anxieties that so many others had known. A bond of sympathy had drawn them closer to the whole nation than any Royal couple had ever been before.

There were signs of the times too within the Abbey; in the lounge suits worn by many of the guests in place of the traditional Court dress or full dress uniform—a concession both to clothes rationing and to postwar economy. Even the bridegroom wore only the everyday uniform of a naval officer, instead of the conventional frock coat and cocked hat of full dress.

The sword he carried was a borrowed one, which had once belonged to his grandfather, Prince Louis of Battenburg, for, like so many officers commissioned during the war, he did not possess one of his own.

The engagement ring which he had given his bride was one that had belonged to his mother and had been re-set; a first lieutenant's pay does not run to diamonds worthy of a King's daughter.

They were beginning married life, this fairy-tale Princess and her tall, handsome husband, as many other young couples in that waiting crowd outside the Abbey had had to begin it—by sharing a home with the in-laws until they could have one of their own. After their return from their honeymoon they were to live temporarily with the King and Queen at Buckingham Palace.

There were many democratic touches in the arrangements for the wedding; in the simplicity of the menu at the reception; in the absence of stands in the Abbey, which would have called for building materials and labor; most of all in the number of people with no special claim to distinction invited by both bride and bridegroom—former shipmates of the Duke's, girls who had served in the A.T.S. with Princess Elizabeth, workers from the Royal estates.

The organ pealed out the hymn chosen by Princess Elizabeth—the 23rd Psalm, in the old Scottish paraphrase, to the tune of Crimond: "The Lord's my Shepherd, I'll not want."

It had been the first hymn that the young Duchess of York had taught her three-year-old daughter to sing. And now that daughter was standing with her tall bridegroom at the altar where she herself had once stood as a bride. But the Queen's eyes, as they rested proudly on her, were untroubled by any thought of parting. She was happy and at peace over Princess Elizabeth, who was marrying the man she loved, as her mother had done.

The honeymoon, part of which was spent at Broadlands, Lord and Lady Mountbatten's house in Hampshire, and the remainder at Birkhall, the Scottish home where Princess Elizabeth had passed some of the happiest days of her childhood, was the last spell of informality the new Duke and Duchess of Edinburgh were to know for a long time, and they made the most of it.

It was fun dodging the cameramen who hung about outside the gates of Broadlands, and driving out into the country lanes in the winter afternoon sunshine, passing little villages where the people turned to stare with mild interest at the tall, good-looking young man at the wheel of a sports car, and the radiant laughing girl in a fur coat and head scarf beside him.

No crowds, no cheers to acknowledge. Only after they had flashed by someone would say, "Wasn't that Princess Elizabeth?" But by that time they would have gone on to the next village to eat a cosy tea in the front parlor of the inn, with a big fire blazing in the hearth and homemade cakes brought in by the innkeeper's wife.

The young husband and wife came back from their honeymoon to face a number of problems. Heading the list was the question of the Duke's future career. In many quarters it was already being suggested that he ought to give up sea-going for good and devote himself to public life. Against this was his own inclination, loyally backed by Princess Elizabeth.

With loving preception she realized how much his heart was set on the ultimate ambition of every naval officer

—an independent command. He would have to serve some years before he could attain it, but it would inevitably come his way. As a naval officer he has always been outstanding.

To have asked him, in those early days of his marriage, to give up for ever his man's world of the sea and the comradeship of the wardroom in exchange for a life of official dinners, prize distributions, and visits to hospitals would have meant frustration for him. The Princess set her face resolutely against it, and succeeded in convincing the King.

The upshot was that the Duke was appointed to temporary duty in the Admiralty with the Director of Operations. It was a routine job, entailing sitting at a desk from nine till five every day, and on Saturdays from nine till one. He nearly always walked there from Buckingham Palace, turning back to wave to Princess Elizabeth as he started down the Mall, like any other young husband.

By then they were living in temporary quarters in Kensington Palace, but the Princess always got up early so that he could drive her down with him and leave her—and the car—at Buckingham Palace before going off to his day's work at the Admiralty. In the evening when he used to call for her again she was always at one of the Palace windows looking out for him.

Whenever it was possible they went down for week ends to Windlesham Moor, the country house near Sunningdale which they had taken on a short lease. It was a pleasant, unpretentious manor with a lovely garden surrounded by a thick screen of trees. In front of the house was a lawn which was immediately marked down by Prince Philip for a rough cricket pitch. He generally managed to get a game on Saturday afternoons with the butler, the gardener, the odd-job man and the policeman on duty, reinforced by the postman and one or two local boys. Before long Princess Elizabeth had to protest that unless the pitch was moved farther away there would not be a single window left intact on the ground floor of the front of the house!

Their happiest hours were spent going round Clarence House, which was to be their London residence as soon as it could be got ready for them. It was a depressing proposition in those days, a gaunt, gloomy building, badly damaged by bombs and in need of cleaning and redecorating throughout. Its new owners—both fond of cooking whenever they get the chance—were dismayed at the sight of the antiquated kitchens, with their absence of any kind of labor-saving devices and their old-fashioned equipment.

"We'll have to get in a new cooker, at least, or else live on sandwiches," decided Prince Philip. "And something will have to be done about the bathroom, even if I have to paint it myself."

Whenever there was an opportunity of getting away to Clarence House together they always seized it, though it sometimes meant slipping away separately and meeting there to dodge the Royal Household officials appointed to help them. It was to be their own home and they wanted to choose the furniture and decorations to suit their own taste, not in accordance with Royal precedent.

At the beginning, their ideas sometimes clashed. Prince Philip was addicted to pale woods, light chintzes, and the minimum of pictures. The Princess had her mother's preference for Chippendale, brocades and watercolors, and was converted only after a struggle.

"Philip is trying to make his study as like a wardroom as possible," she told one of her friends laughingly, "but it's got to stop at that."

But in the end she was won over, and now they have very similar tastes in furnishings.

They loved to potter about Clarence House, planning color schemes, matching up patterns for curtains and cushions, and talking to the painters and carpenters. Sometimes Prince Philip would take off his coat and lend a hand with the furniture moving, while the Princess perched on a packing case and looked on.

By now they were already beginning to talk of "the nursery" and to spend a lot of time in the big light suite of rooms on the second floor. Together, with all the happiness and excitement of any young prospective parents, they chose the corn-flower blue carpet and the cream chintz with its design of nursery-rhyme figures in red.

But most of the time Prince Philip was doing more than a full-time job. At the end of a day's work at the Admiralty he would often come back to an evening of public engagements. Even week ends began to be no longer his own; there was nearly always some meeting to attend or a speech to be prepared.

It was an unsettling life for both of them in those early days, and especially for Prince Philip. Although he was of Royal birth he was new to the obligations of Royalty —the perpetual limelight, the constant need for avoiding anything that could give rise to offense.

This was brought home to him within the first six months of his marriage as the result of the State Visit to

Paris in 1948, when he and Princess Elizabeth were the guests of the President and Mme. Auriol.

The visit was a great success. The susceptible Parisians were enchanted with the Princess, just as they had been enchanted with her mother ten years before. The entire press raved over her lovely skin, her blue eyes, the perfection of her French accent. Prince Philip, by comparison, was not so popular—certainly not half so popular as he would be later in Canada—and since he is sensitive he probably realized it, for he did not play up to the crowds. He never dispenses the conventional smiles generally expected of Royalty; his sincerity stands in the way of that. He smiles when he is genuinely amused or pleased.

He returned to England to face a battery of criticism. Extreme Sabbatarians had been enraged by an incident of the visit to Paris; a clergyman had deplored "the dark day in our history."

What had happened was that the Princess and her husband, arriving in Paris on a Friday, had attended morning service at the British Embassy Church on Sunday, and taken Communion. But for the rest of the day they amused themselves like normal visitors to the French capital. They went in the afternoon to the races at Longchamp—where the Duke backed a winner—and in the evening to a party given by the British Ambassador at a well-known night club, which had been taken over specially for the occasion. Next day the French papers came out with the story, which reached England in a much exaggerated form. Consequently some hard and completely undeserved things were said of two very conscientious young people.

Chapter 12

THE years dealt lightly with the Queen. At forty-eight there was no gray in her untinted hair and her coloring was still the pink and white of the youthful Elizabeth Bowes-Lyon, though it was the year of her Silver Wedding, and before it ended she would be a grandmother. With the King she drove to the Thanksgiving Service at St. Paul's Cathedral on the anniversary of their marriage, and that evening both of them broadcast to the nation.

The King spoke—in that slow voice that had grown familiar to millions in the dark days of the war, and which always carried conviction in spite of its hesitation—of the burden which the years had laid on him.

"There have been times when it would have been too heavy but for the strength and comfort which I have always found in my home," he said.

It was true. Theirs was a perfect marriage. The years had brought them many experiences, had transformed the shy retiring young man who had fallen in love with the daughter of a Scottish earl into a King who was beloved

by his people and respected by the whole world. But behind all that he had achieved stood the figure of the Queen,
his wife. Through the twenty-five years of their marriage
she had always been there to give the encouragement and
security which he needed above all else.

"I'm absolutely lost without her," he said once, lightly,
to his sister-in-law, Lady Granville, when the Queen was in
bed for a few days with influenza. Then he added more
seriously, "It is only when she is not here that I realize
how much I depend on her."

Whenever she was away from home he telephoned to
her at least once a day. There can have been no more
devoted couple in the whole country. Their contentment
was reflected in every aspect of their private life, and most
of all in their children.

Princess Elizabeth's happiness was an echo of their
own. She was beginning to catch something of the gaiety
and spontaneity of the young man she had married. Perhaps that was what had attracted her to him in the first
place. Although she was young when he first entered her
world, her life had already held much sober self-discipline.
She had often listened to the weighty conversation of
statesmen instead of amusing herself with people of her
own age. Even the young men and girls in the restricted
Royal circle, who played with her as children and grew up
with her, always deferred to her, making her seem in a sub-
tle way much older than themselves. Prince Philip treated
her just like any other girl. He was human and completely
natural and expected her to be the same.

He brought her a sense of freedom. He teased her—a
thing none had ever done before—and he took her outside

herself into a world that was quite new to her. She loved
to hear about his life at sea. He tells a story exceptionally
well and is a born mimic. Very often at informal dinners
with the Royal Family at Windsor he would send King
George VI and everyone else at the table into fits of laughter by taking off some of the men who had served with
him.

In the early days of his marriage his independent outlook often brought him into conflicts with the tradition
that envelops Royalty from the cradle to the grave, and
which is always quoted as the final authority in any argu-
ment. Because this or that had been an institution at Buckingham Palace since the beginning of Queen Victoria's
reign, he saw no reason why it should continue to be, and
he did not hesitate to say so.

There was, for instance, the appointment of Commander Parker as his first equerry. Michael Parker was an
Australian, an unknown naval officer with apparently no
special qualifications for the job beyond the fact that he
had met Prince Philip on active service during the war and
had become one of his friends.

Such appointments had always been filled by the sons
of members of the Royal Household or by those within the
immediate circle of the Court. A man from overseas, it
was pointed out, would lack the necessary background and
experience and could not be expected to fill the role satis-
factorily. But Prince Philip—again loyally supported by
Princess Elizabeth—insisted that Michael Parker was the
right man for the job, and Michael Parker got it. Today
he is the Duke of Edinburgh's Private Secretary, and in

addition one of the most efficient and best-liked men in the circle around the Throne.

Prince Philip's informality did not always commend itself to the older generation, particularly where it affected Princess Elizabeth. There were raised eyebrows when he attended a fancy dress ball at the American Embassy disguised as a waiter, with Princess Elizabeth disguised as a waitress. Queen Victoria and Albert the Good would not in their wildest moments have been guilty of such a descent from dignity!

They would not. Nor would they have paid an informal visit to the House of Commons together and sat through a debate; or visited magistrates' courts and boys' clubs and factories, to mix with people of all types, not as Royalty from behind an impenetrable screen of formality, but as two genuinely interested people.

By that time even his critics had to admit that Prince Philip was making a success of public life. He had adapted himself to the difficult role of husband of the Heir Apparent with great tact, but without sacrificing his own personality. His influence was increasing in many fields. He was throwing himself, with the inexhaustible energy which is one of his chief assets, into a wide range of activities. When he was not touring the provinces with Princess Elizabeth, he was sitting on committees, inspecting factories, laying foundation stones, or presiding at meetings of the National Playing Fields Association. His engagements multiplied so fast that every page of his diary was filled weeks ahead.

In the autumn of 1948 all those around him noticed that the King was looking haggard and ill. The Queen worried increasingly over him. But Princess Elizabeth was expecting her first baby, and her father did not want to detract from her happiness. So the Queen tried to stifle her anxiety and to concentrate on preparations for the arrival of her grandchild. The pram, which had been her own children's, was got out again and reconditioned; the cot and the baby's basket were fetched out of the cupboard where they had lain for years, and relined. The Queen knitted a set of woollies for the baby, and took a grandmother's interest in the plans for the nursery which the Princess and the Duke had decided upon for their new home, Clarence House.

On November 14, 1948, Prince Charles was born. He was a lovely baby as his mother had been. "I wished so much that Alah had lived to see him," the Queen said to her sister Lady Granville.

Her own happiness in the birth of her first grandchild was cut short by the news that the King was seriously ill, suffering from an obstruction to the circulation through the arteries of the legs. All engagements had to be cancelled. The tour of Australia, planned for the following spring, was indefinitely postponed.

The next few months were anxious ones for the entire Royal Family, and most of all for the Queen. An operation for lumbar sympathectomy was performed on the King in March, 1949. It was successful, even though he was the worst of patients. He fought against his illness as he had done years before in his boyhood. No sooner was the operation over than he was sitting up dealing with State papers. The Queen, who spent many hours of the day with him, would come into the room and find the contents of his dispatch boxes littered over the bed.

Gradually he recovered, and in the summer life resumed its normal course. The family gathering at Balmoral in August was a specially happy one, with the old nursery in use again for Prince Charles. Princess Elizabeth loved to wheel her baby out in his pram, and very often her mother and Princess Margaret went with her, taking a picnic tea with them, while the King was out shooting. It was still the simple home life of a generation earlier, when the young Duchess of York had walked with her children in the woods.

A year later, in August, 1950, Princess Anne was born, and this second grandchild completed the family circle. "Sometimes I think I'm almost too happy," the Queen said to one of her friends.

Both for her and for the King this was the time of harvest, the fruits of the long years of service. Even while monarchy throughout the world was at a lower premium than ever before in history, the King of England was secure in the love of the entire nation. During his illness thousands had crowded round the gates of Buckingham Palace, waiting for the next bulletin; those same Londoners who had once chanted outside 145 Piccadilly, "We want King Edward."

For the Queen especially that year of 1950 had been one of fulfilment, for with the strain of the King's illness receding into the background, she had been able to revive many of her own interests which had been shelved during the war. Her influence was once again making itself felt in the world of art and music.

Born of a family which has produced several painters of talent, and initiated in art by a mother who was one of the noted connoisseurs of her generation, she has been passionately fond of pictures since her childhood. Her own personal collection took shape in the early years of her marriage and she has been adding to it ever since. As a collector she has preference for modern works—Graham Sutherland and Augustus John are her favorite painters— and probably no Queen Consort, with the possible exception of Queen Mary, has ever given so much encouragement to contemporary art. In the months following the King's recovery she was able to devote time to the rearrangement of the Royal art collections at Buckingham Palace and Windsor Castle, which had suffered as the result of the war, visit a number of exhibitions, and commission new pictures.

At fifty she could still bring enthusiasm, vitality, and freshness of outlook to public life. Her influence as Queen Consort was as stimulating as it had been in the home circle of the Royal Family in the early days of her marriage. Her imagination had enabled her to keep in step with the general trend of thought beyond the gates of a palace, and to depend on her own intuition rather than on tradition or precedent.

Her pioneering spirit, backed by the King's leaning toward simplicity, was shown in the many practical innovations of their reign. In the curtailing of ceremonial procedure and the scrapping of many obsolete institutions of Court life; in the substitution of dark blue battle-dress for the Royal servants in place of the elaborate uniforms of the past. In the Garden Parties that were so representative of the democracy of "The People's King and Queen," where the guests might include miners and their wives from the north, or a contingent of overseas schoolteachers; and where formality had given place to friendliness.

In the summer of 1951 the King and Queen went up to Balmoral as usual. The purple-clad moors were as peaceful as ever; the cry of the curlews was the same. There was the happy family gathering; friends of Princess Margaret came to stay; Princess Elizabeth and Prince Philip were at Birkhall with their children. The King went shooting with his keepers, spending long days on the moors. But the Queen could not rest. To her loving observation the King's face had changed. He did not look well.

He had had a comparatively mild attack of influenza in the early summer, and a week later his doctors had discovered a small inflamed patch on one lung. It had subsided after treatment, although he had been forced to cut down the heavy program of public engagements which had been piling up since the beginning of the year. He had refused to admit that there was anything wrong with his health that a few weeks of Balmoral air would not cure.

The Queen, knowing that he hated nothing so much as to be fussed over, worried only in secret. But when he continued to lose weight steadily, in spite of the rest and the air, and her persistent efforts to feed him up, she could no longer hide her anxiety. She begged him to ask his doctors to come up to Balmoral to give him a complete checkup.

When he learned the truth, after the X-ray examination for which he went up to London, he did not conceal it from her. All through their marriage they had faced every

ordeal together. Her one thought now was to help him.
He had always relied on her and this was the supreme test
of her love. Knowing, with the sensitive intuition that had
always enabled her to smooth the path for him, how much
support her confidence could give him, she showed no
hint of the strain which she was undergoing.

In the days after his operation in September she
scarcely left his bedside except for short intervals, for although four nurses were in attendance on him, he always
wanted her to be somewhere near. She cancelled all her
private engagements and cut down her public duties to a
minimum so that she could give all her time to him. In
those weeks of suspense she never allowed her anxiety to
rob her smile of its brightness.

Although the King had apparently made a complete
recovery after his operation, neither he nor she were deceived over his health. As Winston Churchill was to say
afterward, "The King walked with death as if death were a
companion, an acquaintance whom he recognized and did
not fear." The Queen, with whom he had shared every joy
and sorrow for more than twenty-five years, shared this
knowledge too. But by a tacit understanding they never
talked of the shadow that hung over them.

Both of them kept up the gallant pretense that all was
well, and the King worked harder than ever to make up for
the time lost during his illness. He would only very rarely
let the Queen deputize for him. He insisted on making his
customary broadcast on Christmas Day, although for the
first time it had to be recorded. He laughed at his doctors
when they tried to dissuade him, and suggested that Prin-

cess Elizabeth should read his message to the nation, to spare him the strain.

"I've always broadcast myself," he said, "and I'm quite well enough to do it now."

The broadcast, which went to the hearts of so many listeners, because something of the effort behind it came across the air, was one of the most cheerful he ever made. "Christmas is, and always will be, a time when we can and should count our blessings—the blessings of home, the blessings of happy gatherings, and the blessings of the hopeful message of Christmas."

And so the days passed to that first week in February, 1952. The King was beginning to look more like himself than he had done for some time. The immediate need for anxiety seemed to be over. Princess Elizabeth had just left with the Duke of Edinburgh for Kenya before starting on a Royal tour of Australia and New Zealand. The King had given her a movie camera for the trip to the National Park in Nairobi. "Mind you get a lion with it," he told her. He was still the best photographer in the family, although both the Princesses and Prince Philip were far above the average amateur. His eyes were filled with pride as he stood at London Airport, waving a gay farewell to the loved daughter whom he had trained so carefully to succeed him. Then he went back to Sandringham for a few days; to the broad fields and woods of his Norfolk estate, where he was less of a king than a country squire, surrounded by tenants who were his friends.

February 5 was a typically lovely East Anglian day, with the breeze coming in from the sea. He spent most of it shooting with friends, and brought home a big bag. He

had never been in better form. Before dinner he slipped up-
stair to the nursery for a few minutes with Prince Charles
and Princess Anne, who were staying there as usual while
their mother was away.

Princess Anne had gone to bed but Prince Charles was
wide awake and waiting to play soldiers with him. He had
had a whole regiment of toy soldiers given him for Christmas, and in his view his grandfather was the only person
who knew the right order of battle. They set them out to
their satisfaction, and then the King went to change for
dinner.

"I shan't let anyone touch them till you come tomorrow, then we'll play with them again," Prince Charles
called after him. "You will come, won't you?"

"Yes, I'll come tomorrow," the King promised.

The evening was like so many at Sandringham; just
one of the quiet family evenings that the King loved. He
solved his crossword puzzle while the Queen played
patience, and Princess Margaret sang to them both.

The King looked almost well when he went up to bed
talking of plans for the next morning. He was pleasantly
tired after the day's shooting, and so fell asleep. When
morning came he still slept on. For him there was "another
dawn than ours."

Chapter *13*

THE Queen who was born Elizabeth Bowes-Lyon, daughter of a fighting race, has always been known for her courage. Members of her own family and friends who can look back to her childhood at Glamis still picture her as a tiny figure, fearlessly setting her horse at jumps far too high for her, making light of falls. She had always tears to shed in those days for the birds beaten by the storm, or the rabbits snared in the woods, but her brother David remembers seeing her cry only once for any personal sorrow, and that was when he received a caning from his father. In every catastrophe of their childhood, she was always the comforter.

As the child, so the Queen. Even on that February morning when she stood beside the bed of the husband around whom her whole life had centered for nearly thirty years, and knew that he had passed beyond the reach of her love, her thoughts were for others. All through that first week of sorrow her courage sustained the whole family,

191

from the young Queen, called back from Kenya to take up the burden, to Queen Mary, stunned by this new blow.

Of that little group which had known George VI not as Sovereign but as beloved husband, son, and father, only his widow had not been bred in the Royal tradition which exacts the sinking of personal grief in the public ceremonial expected by a mourning nation. The ordeal must have been doubly hard for her: the journey from Sandringham to London, with a battery of press cameras awaiting the train; the procession to Westminster Hall, through streets lined by silent crowds; the solemn lying-in state; the burial at St. George's Chapel. Until the last moment, when the King's coffin was lowered into the vault, the Royal obligations which had for so long ordered his life claimed him from the woman who had been first his wife and then his Queen. The sonorous roll of the titles George VI had borne, proclaimed by the Garter King of Arms at the graveside, had so little relation to the Bertie who had loved Elizabeth Bowes-Lyon. Perhaps the memory of that love sustained her through those days of public mourning, for her rigid self-control never deserted her. It was only when the last Royal duty had been discharged that she could slip away to old friends in the country, to grieve in seclusion.

In the first few weeks of her grief she took refuge in solitude. She turned for comfort to the static things of her childhood; to the beauty and peace of her native Scottish hills; to her garden and her dogs. But after a while she set about quietly reconstructing her life, with courage inspired by her firm religious faith, and with the practical common sense which has always been characteristic of her. While many people were wondering how she would face the lonely years ahead, after more than a quarter of a century passed in the close companionship of a perfect marriage, those who knew her most intimately believed that the future still held a great deal of happiness for her. She is too deeply versed in the art of living, and too much wrapped up in her children's lives to be left without interests.

She has always shown her adaptability in the self-effacing role of Queen Dowager—a far more difficult one to a personality as vital and still youthful as hers than it had been to Queen Alexandra and Queen Mary, who were much older when they were relegated to it. No one who knows the Queen Mother could visualize her as spending the rest of her days in an armchair—least of all the Queen, who has the greatest confidence in her ability.

King George VI set a precedent for his family in giving his wife a place which was probably higher than that held by any Queen Consort in the past. With the same courtesy which prompted him to order a separate procession for Queen Mary at his Coronation, he emphasized the feminine privilege of his Consort by making her precede him when they attended any public function together, a departure from the tradition of both his father and grandfather. He was careful to include a reference to his Queen in all his broadcasts and important speeches, and to identify her in every way with himself. He had no hesitation in owning that he was often influenced by her judgment.

"Your mother is something more than merely clever. She's wise," he used to tell his daughters.

The Queen Mother's interests have always covered a

wide field; her only regret in the past was that she had so little time to give to them. After the King's death she began to take up one by one many of the threads that had had to be dropped during her active public life as Queen Consort; visiting art galleries, no longer officially, but slipping in quietly with Princess Margaret; attending concerts and an occasional theatre or ballet; reading books ordered years ago and put aside. Most of all she has found consolation in the friendships of her youth. She has a large circle of friends, nearly all of them of many years' standing. In the first twelve months of her widowhood she spent much of her time in visiting them, going from one house to another, without any fuss, insisting that no special preparations should be made for her.

Her youngest brother, David, the inseparable companion of her nursery days, is still her closest friend. Even in the years when her life was crowded with public duties, they used to go out together from time to time, to a theatre or a quiet dinner, reviving memories of those days in the First World War when they had pooled their pocket money and stood in line for general admission. Now the Queen Mother goes to spend week ends with her brother at the Hertfordshire home—St. Paul's Waldenbury—which is so dear both to them and to the Queen and Princess Margaret who stayed there very often in their childhood. They are still devoted to this youngest uncle, who is now one of Prince Charles' godfathers.

Since the Coronation the Queen Mother has been taking on more and more public engagements. It was obvious to all who knew her that during the first year of her widowhood she was deliberately effacing herself, reverting without any bitterness from the role of Queen to the simpler pattern of life of the Duchess of York, or even of the earlier Lady Elizabeth Bowes-Lyon. She has never had any real liking for pomp and ceremony: she accepted them, as King George VI did, as essential to the high office to which they had both been called. Although her life has changed so often, and so dramatically, she has never been greatly influenced by circumstances. She has always been able to adapt herself to her surroundings. She told one of her friends quite recently that she could be happy almost anywhere in the country, as long as she had a dog about the house, plenty of books to read, and a garden to work in.

It was the young Queen who prevented her from slipping quietly into the background. With loving intuition she devised new interests for her mother, engagements which could be carried out with practically no publicity, but which would gradually draw her back into public life. Visits to flower shows, to schools, to a home for retired clergymen, and one or two hospitals, paved the way for the round of official entertaining in connection with the Coronation, and the visit to Southern Rhodesia in the summer of 1953.

At first the return to what must have seemed the pale shadow of her life as Consort demanded all the Queen Mother's courage. As she stepped into the *Comet* that was to carry her and Princess Margaret to Rhodesia, the contrast between this and those other overseas visits, when the King had been beside her, must have brought home to her anew the realization of her loneliness. Yet she talked with her usual vivacity to the officials who saw her off, and waved a gay goodbye from the door of the aircraft.

The visit to Rhodesia, with its sequence of public functions, including the opening of the Rhodes Centenary Exhibition, cemented new bonds of friendship. The Royal visitors were received with tremendous enthusiasm everywhere. But although Princess Margaret charmed the crowds with her beauty, and with the glamour that has always surrounded her, it was the fifty-three-year-old Queen Mother who won all hearts. Those who had expected to pity her in her widowhood found themselves marveling at her quiet serenity, and her evident enjoyment of every incident.

This deep tranquility of mind, and the art of creating happiness for herself and for those around her, and of getting the very best out of any existing circumstances, are fundamental in the Queen Mother's character. Her gaiety is as unquenchable now, in her fifties, as in the days when it first charmed the Duke of York. She has still the same capacity for enjoyment. That is perhaps one of the secrets of her appeal to all young people, and most of all to her own daughters.

The family circle of which she has always been the center has been widened now to include the Duke of Edinburgh and Prince Charles and Princess Anne. The Duke has no more loyal friend than his mother-in-law. Marriage with a daughter so devoted to her parents as the Queen might easily have presented difficulties, but from the very beginning he was accepted into the family circle.

The Queen Mother has perhaps given him all the more affection because he has been able to see so little of his own mother since she took the veil, and became Mother Superior of the Convent of the Order of Martha and Mary outside Athens.

The Queen Mother's influence is still as strong in the lives of the Queen and Princess Margaret as it was in their childhood. It will have a bearing on the future of the new generation, for the Queen brings up her children on the lines of her own home. The imprint of the Queen Mother's happy, cosy upbringing at Glamis and St. Paul's Walden-bury was vivid enough to withstand Royal tradition. The normal atmosphere in which her daughters were reared was revolutionary by the standards of Buckingham Palace. Queen Victoria's sons and daughters had been banished to the seclusion of the nurseries and required to send a formal request for an audience with their mother when they wanted to see her. And neither King Edward VII nor King George V—both good fathers in the accepted sense—had ever been known to play with their offspring in their early years. It was left to Lilibet and Margaret, daughters of a young and laughter-loving mother, who had been brought up as a commoner in the informality of a big family, to break down the barrier between Royal parents and their children. They did it effectively, and probably for all time.

The Queen Mother's pattern in home-making is being followed as closely as possible by the young Queen, and consequently both she and Prince Philip contrive even now to see a great deal more of their children than many middle-class parents who are in jobs all day. Every morning begins for Prince Charles and Princess Anne with an hour in "Mummy's Room"—the familiar institution of the Queen's own childhood which was continued right on until the time of her marriage—and every evening ends with a romp, always with their mother, and very often with both parents. Any odd moments that the Queen can spare during the day are also given to them. A friend of the Royal Family told me that it was charming to see her, at the end of a long morning's work on affairs of State, suddenly sprinting upstairs to the nursery for ten minutes' play with her children before lunch.

The determination of the Duke and Duchess of York to give their children a normal childhood, free of any Royal obligations until they were old enough to understand them, is echoed by the Queen and the Duke of Edinburgh today. Both of them have resolved not to allow Prince Charles or Princess Anne to make any kind of public appearance. Hundreds of applications come in during the year asking for their names to be enrolled as members or patrons of various societies, but they are always refused. When an approach was made only recently for Prince Charles to become one of the sponsors of a world-famous organization, it was suggested that an exception might be made, but the Duke of Edinburgh was adamant.

"How are we to know whether Charles will even be interested in that sort of thing when he grows up?" he pointed out. "It would be unfair of us to commit him to it now."

The one and only exception was made when Princess Anne was registered as the millionth member of the A.A. Both her parents agreed that they were on safe ground there, as every normal girl is interested in motoring!

Both children are encouraged to make friends with other boys and girls. Several members of the Queen's entourage have children of about the same age, so there are plenty of opportunities for getting together. And if a quarrel breaks out, as quarrels have a way of breaking out in all nurseries, there is no rush of anxious nannies to save Royal dignity.

Although they wave to crowds automatically, because they have been taught to do it from their earliest babyhood, they are never allowed to feel that they are in any way different from other children.

To them their parents are not the Queen and the Prince Consort but simply Mummy and Papa, who romp with them like any other young parents, and love nothing better than to take them out for picnics.

The Duke is determined to make his son an all-around athlete like himself. He has already bought him a miniature cricket bat and a soft football, taught him to ride a bicycle, and given him his first swimming lessons. Although it is still too early for any definite plans for Prince Charles' education his father is strongly in favor of a public school for him. He wants him to mix with other boys—as he himself did—on an equal footing. And if he gets his way, the Heir to the Throne will probably prove as good a mixer as the former Prince Philip of Greece was, for there is much in common in their characters.

Prince Charles is already showing that he has inherited his father's inquiring mind and keen observation; a fact which delighted Kurt Hahn, the Duke's old headmaster, when he paid a visit to Balmoral in the summer of 1952. He drove up from Gordonstoun in the school car, which became an immediate object of interest to Prince Charles when he trotted out to the front door after his father, to bid goodbye to the visitor. After walking round and round the car, examining it with a critical eye, he turned to the Duke of Edinburgh delightedly.

"Papa, Mr. Hahn has come in a taxi. How did he get it? Did he bring it all the way from London?"

"Good for you, son," said his father. "It is a taxi, but it hasn't come from London. Mr. Hahn likes taxis so much that the school gave him one for himself."

It was true. The school car had actually begun its existence as a taxi, but it took the keen observation of a three-and-a-half-year-old, fascinated by cars of every description, to register the fact.

Both the Queen and the Duke of Edinburgh share the same determination to have their children brought up with the minimum of rules and regulations. They are never confined to the nursery quarters even at Buckingham Palace, and wander in and out of their parents' rooms and talk to visitors in the most natural way.

Prince Charles often invades his father's study for ten minutes' play during the morning, and unless the Duke is working hard, he is never chased out. More than one official visitor who has called has found a toy motor left on the desk, or a picture book still lying open on the floor.

The Queen Mother has a prominent place in the lives of her two small grandchildren. Prince Charles especially is devoted to her. Nothing makes him happier than to be allowed to work beside her in the garden when he goes to stay with her at Royal Lodge. With the miniature set of tools and garden roller which she has given him he can imitate her. She still laughs over the memory of the day when she was so absorbed in her own weeding that she did not pay much attention to his efforts. Before she realized what he was doing he had zealously uprooted a whole bed of newly planted annuals! Since then she has directed his energies into safer channels. She has already given him his first paint-box and taken him to his first concert—one of the ones to which she used to take her own children years ago.

She has been pleased at the discovery that he has his mother's quick ear for music. He has already a definite sense of rhythm and can sing a number of nursery rhymes, the favorite of the moment being "The Grand Old Duke of York," which he picked up from the B.B.C. "Listen With Mother" program. He marches round the nursery to the tune, followed by Princess Anne and anyone else who can be recruited.

Both the children love martial music of any sort, with a preference for bagpipes. Prince Charles, like most small boys, has a passion for anything military, and his sister has caught it from him. They are so close in age that she models herself on him, copies all his expressions and leaves her own dolls to play with his soldiers and clockwork trains. This occasionally leads to strained relations, for although Charles is very fond of his little sister, and has a tolerant protective way with her—as his mother had in her childhood with Princess Margaret—he is getting to the stage of wanting to shake her off sometimes and gang up with his father as the men of the family.

Once when she took possession of his favorite toy motorcar, and refused to give it up, he tried peaceful persuasion at first, but when that failed he suddenly lost patience and snatched it from her.

Nurse Lightbody—the Alah of this new generation—was shocked; so were the two Scottish nursery maids. Even his indulgent Granny, the Queen Mother, shook her head when she came into the nursery and heard that Charles had made his baby sister cry. So a rather dejected little boy took his remorse into a corner and sat there until the Duke of Edinburgh appeared at the door.

His son rushed up to him with relief and slipped a hand into his. "Papa," he said earnestly, "let's go out somewhere, and get away from all these girls."

The family holidays instituted by the Queen Mother when as the young Duchess of York she gave up most of the days at Birkhall to her children, and made a point of looking after them herself as much as possible, are becoming a tradition with the Queen and the Duke of Edinburgh. At Balmoral last summer they used to take the children out nearly every afternoon, without nursery maids or any members of their Household, though the party would usually include the Queen Mother and Princess Margaret when they were staying at the Castle. The favorite plan was to pile into the shooting brake, with the Duke of Edinburgh at the wheel, and drive off for a picnic. To anyone meeting them on the road they looked just an ordinary, happy middle-class family on holiday.

The Queen has her mother's inclination toward simplicity. She enjoyed probably more than anything in her life the time she spent as a young bride in Malta when the Duke of Edinburgh was stationed there with the Mediterranean Fleet.

Leading the ordinary everyday life of the British colony on the island, just one among the other officers' wives who were out there with their husbands, she could forget her Royal rank. For the first time in her memory there were no crowds in the street to stare at her. She drove all over the island in her little car, generally unrecognized. Once she got into trouble with a Maltese policeman for parking in a forbidden place and had to give her name and address. She did all her own shopping, interviewed the cook every morning at the villa where she stayed, and ordered the day's meals. She went over Prince Philip's wardrobe, decided that he needed new shirts and bought them herself and took his suits to the cleaners when it was necessary.

She soon learned to know her way about the island and found the best shops. She had her hair shampooed and set by the local hairdresser, and went to his little shop like everyone else instead of having him come to the villa. The other officers' wives accepted her from the start with simple friendliness as one of themselves. She liked their informality and was both pleased and amused when she discovered that they called her "Liz" among themselves.

By the time the Duke of Edinburgh was appointed to the command of the frigate *Magpie*, she had fallen into the ways of the Navy.

"You'll have to give the usual party that the captain's wife always gives for the other wives on the day the ship sails, darling," Prince Philip told her when the *Magpie* was due to leave with other ships of the Mediterranean Fleet on anti-submarine exercises.

"Of course I will. I'd love to," she said at once.

So the wives were entertained to tea at the villa. They still remember what a charming hostess the Princess was, and how unaffectedly she made the tea herself.

Those days in Malta were profoundly happy for her, perhaps some of the happiest in her life. Looking back on them she told one of her friends, "I used to wish that time could have stood still."

Motherhood has drawn the Queen even closer to her own mother, for they share the same interest in the upbringing of Prince Charles and Princess Anne. The happiness of her own childhood has proved to the young Queen that it is possible to reconcile a life of public service with the rearing of a family on normal lines, but even so it is a comfort to her to know that she need have no anxiety for her children when she is far away from them on an overseas tour, since their grandmother is always at hand to take charge. Already both children are quite as much at home at Clarence House or Royal Lodge as at Buckingham Palace.

"I don't think my son is in any special hurry for me to get back to England," the Queen told a member of her suite during her Australian tour in the spring of 1954. "What can you expect when he has an adoring Granny to spoil him? He doesn't get quite so much of his own way when he has his father and me to reckon with!"

Chapter *14*

THE happiest family reunions are at Royal Lodge, which is still the Queen Mother's favorite home. She spends most week ends there with Princess Margaret, and very often they are joined by the Queen and the Duke of Edinburgh, who come down by car from London on Saturday afternoon, and leave the following evening. They can rarely get a whole week end there, for both of them start their working week early on Monday morning. When the children go down too—ahead of their parents with Nurse Lightbody—the circle is complete. The Queen and Princess Margaret revive their own childhood playing in "The Little House" with Prince Charles who is just growing old enough to appreciate it, although he finds the water taps and various electrical gadgets too fascinating to be allowed a free hand there.

For the Queen Mother, Royal Lodge is a house of memories for it represented, more than any other, home to her and to King George. Every room has its associations—the furniture which they chose together; well-worn possessions which the King liked to have around him; toys the children played with.

The garden, in its present form, is of the Queen Mother's own creation. It had been neglected for many years before she took it in hand, reclaiming it bit by bit from the weeds and laying it out again to her own design. Walking among the rose trees which she and King George planted together, her corgis at her heels, she can recapture the glow of those days before the war when a young father and mother raced their little girls along the paths.

She has still the same pleasure in creating a home around her. Nothing interests her more than taking over a house or garden and adapting it to her own individual ideas. She has already effected the transformation of the rambling old Castle of Mey, her Scottish home on the shore of Caithness, and somehow contrived to bring life and warmth to its gloomy interior, even though she has only found time to stay there once or twice.

Clarence House, too, soon showed the imprint of her personality. Although the Queen and the Duke of Edinburgh had it modernized in many ways, particularly in regard to the kitchens and household equipment, a good deal of adjustment has been necessary. In spite of its size there are actually very few rooms, a disadvantage which was easily overcome in the case of a husband and wife, but which presents more problems to a mother and daughter each needing a separate suite. There has been extensive redecorating too, for the Queen and her mother, who have so many things in common, have totally different ideas on furnishing.

Both the Queen and the Duke of Edinburgh like modern furniture, pale woods, and the minimum of decoration. The Queen Mother prefers the darker, more traditional setting of period pieces and, above all, pictures. One of the first things she did on taking over Clarence House was to remove the peeled walnut panelling in the Duke of Edinburgh's sitting room, though the Queen had been particularly proud of it.

With all the official entertaining which she will undertake to help the Queen, an increasing number of public engagements, overseas travel, and the running of a home for herself and Princess Margaret, the Queen Mother's life will be a very full one in the future. This is her own choice, for the adventurous streak in her character makes her love new experiences and meeting new people. She is interested in everything and everybody.

"Most people are charmed by the Queen Mother," one of her friends told me, "but very few people outside her own family circle really know her. Her character has so many facets. At one moment she is serious—passionately serious—over something that she feels deeply, such as cruelty to children. At the next she is laughing with Princess Margaret, talking to her like a sister rather than like a mother."

The similarity of their tastes makes the Queen Mother and her younger daughter perfect companions. Both have the same love of fun and gift for mimicry. Both are keenly interested in music, art and the theatre. Both can enjoy a country walk although they do not care for outdoor sports as much as the Queen does.

The bond of sympathy between them has become closer since the King died. For some time Princess Margaret grieved so desperately over this first real sorrow in her life that her mother grew anxious for her health and did everything in her power to provide distractions for her. She herself had resignation, and the comfort of a religious faith strengthened by the years. The Queen had her husband and children to turn to. Princess Margaret alone took the full force of the blow.

She had always been devoted to her father. Even as a small child, naturally mischievous and high-spirited, she would do anything to please him. Alah used to tell the story of one summer afternoon at Royal Lodge when the two little Princesses went downstairs to play with their parents. When the game was over the Duke of York—as he was in those days—took out the plans of some rebuilding he was having done on the estate and began to study them. This did not please the four-year-old Margaret, who wanted her father to go on playing with her. After several unsuccessful attempts to get his undivided attention, she suddenly lost her temper, seized the plans and tore them in two.

The Duke reacted like any other exasperated father. He picked up his small daughter, turned her upside down, and administered a sharp slap. It was the first time in her short life that such a thing had ever happened to her, and her dignity suffered badly. Without a word she crept out of the room and upstairs to the nursery, where Alah found her a few minutes later, sitting in the middle of the floor, too surprised to cry.

It was obvious that her small world had crashed around her, but Alah, who had nursed two generations of children, was wise enough not to ask for explanations. Presently a whisper came from the little figure on the floor. "Alah, something dreadful has happened. Papa smacked me!"

The old nurse shook her head. "Then all I can say is

that you must have been very, very naughty to make Papa lose his temper with you. I think you should go straight back to him, and tell him you're sorry."

Pride dies hard, even at four years old, and hour after hour passed without any sign of repentance. But as the evening shadows fell and bedtime came round the Princess suddenly burst into tears and rushed downstairs to fling herself into her father's arms and ask for forgiveness.

She came back to the nursery all smiles and good resolutions. That night a new petition was added to her bedtime prayers: "Please God, never let me make Papa angry again."

She never did. All through his latter years she was his greatest source of happiness. He understood her as it is given to few fathers to understand their children. She recalled so vividly to him the young Elizabeth Bowes-Lyon with whom he had fallen in love. He knew that the same gaiety and mischievous wit which had charmed him in the past hid in Princess Margaret, as in her mother, emotional depths unsuspected by most people. At the end of a long and tiring day he could always find relaxation in her society.

Nothing annoyed him more than the attacks made on her in the foreign press, for he knew, probably better than anyone else, how unjustified they were. Few girls have been more maligned than the younger sister who was just growing up at the time of Princess Elizabeth's marriage.

The picture created by some of the newspapers of a spoilt and undisciplined child always in search of excitement, living for parties and rarely spending an evening at home, was an entirely false one, as all those closely associated with her knew. In reality Princess Margaret was very

lonely in those first months of being the unmarried daughter at the Palace. Since her earliest childhood, she and
Princess Elizabeth had been inseparable. They had done
everything together, and neither had felt the need of outside friendships. But now the elder sister, who had always
taken the lead in everything, had a husband and new interests, and the younger was left to reorganize her whole
life.

It was actually the Queen who was the first to realize
her loneliness and to suggest that she should start going out
more with parties of other young people, and also invite
her own friends to Sandringham and Balmoral. Then as
she grew older she began to find new interests. She took on
many more public duties, and carried them out very well.
She worked hard at her music, and after a while she formed
her own group of friends, and found her own amusements
—like any normal girl of her age.

The King and Queen saw no reason why she should
not go to theatres and dances, and even to public restau-
rants, attended by her lady-in-waiting, and with other young
people. But she has never led the hectic social life with
which she has been credited. In reality many a career girl
went out more evenings in a month than Princess Margaret did.

Recently, one of the Princess' closest friends told
me of a letter which she had received from her, which re-
veals infinitely more of the real Margaret than anything
that has ever been published about her.

It was written soon after the Princess' visit to Paris in
the summer of 1949, when the killjoys were scandalized by
reports of her dancing at the British Embassy until 3 A.M.

on a Sunday morning, overlooking in their indignation the fact that she had attended service at the Embassy Church a few hours later. A particularly offensive article which had appeared in one of the foreign newspapers had reached the eyes of the Princess. Commenting on it in her letter to this friend, who had known her since her childhood she wrote:

> It is a horrible picture of my character. To say that I am interested in nothing but dancing and young men is unjust. Does not every normal girl of my age like dancing? And isn't it only natural for a young woman to be interested in men, and to look forward to the day when she will fall in love and have a husband and children of her own?

That is perhaps the key to all the gossip and speculation which have always surrounded Princess Margaret from the day she put on her first long dress. Neither the press nor the public will accept her as the completely natural normal young woman that she is. If she had been born into a middle-class home, even the most conventional neighbors would have found little to criticize in her, so much is she the reflection of her own generation. She has the freedom of thought and uninhibited self-expression of all her contemporaries, whereas in the past British Royalty has been anything but free.

Take the question of her smoking. Any career girl can enjoy a cigarette over her lunch in a restaurant without arousing comments, but when Princess Margaret smokes in public—using a long cigarette holder like her aunt, the Duchess of Kent—the self-righteous are shocked. Royal ladies have smoked in the past, but not openly. One of the most beloved was so afraid of being detected in the practice that she used to hide her lighted cigarette behind her back when any members of her Household entered the room, and converse with them regardless of the fact that clouds of smoke were appearing over her shoulder. But the Princess, who was only a child of nine when the Second World War broke out, is too transparently honest in her way of thinking to concede to hypocrisy. She wants to smoke and she smokes.

It is the same with all her pleasures. She has outgrown the phase of night clubs, although she goes to one occasionally, with a party of friends after the theatre. When she is there she enjoys herself like any other girl, dances every dance, and drinks champagne in moderation. She prefers a private dance or small dinner party at the house of an intimate friend—most of all an evening at the theatre or ballet. Her tastes are in reality rather quiet. She likes reading, good conversation, attending lectures, listening to the B.B.C. Third Program. She has her own sitting room at Clarence House, and there she often entertains her friends, generally to informal snacks before the theatre.

The Princess has her mother's fidelity in friendship. Most of the young people in her own circle are the friends who played with her as children. Many of them are married now. Lady Caroline Scott, who shared her first dancing classes, is the wife of Mr. Ian Gilmour. Miss Laura Smith, who was the Princess' closest companion in the dark days after the death of King George VI, is now Mrs. Michael Brand. Lady Rosemary Spencer-Churchill, another playmate of nursery days, is married to Mr. Robin Muir.

Then there is the string of young men, each one of whom was hailed in turn by popular fallacy as Princess Margaret's fiancé—Lord Blandford, Lord Dalkeith, Lord Ogilvy —who have said goodbye to their bachelor days. Princess Margaret has attended their weddings, one after another, welcomed their wives into her own intimate set, and visited their homes. One of those who has become most friendly with her is Lady Ogilvy, the American-born Miss Virginia Ryan.

The Princess has always had a special liking for American girls, dating back to her first friendship with Sharman Douglas, the daughter of the former Ambassador to Britain. The Queen Mother shares this, and, in spite of the lapse of time, has kept a warm place in her heart for the entire Douglas family. Whenever they are in England they are always invited to visit her. Lady Astor is another of the Queen Mother's American-born women friends, and one for whose courage and energy she has a very great admiration.

But the American woman who has made the deepest impression on her is Mrs. Franklin D. Roosevelt. The bond between the widowed Queen and the widow of the President, whose name became in Britain the symbol of American friendship, is one of mutual affection and esteem. It was formed during the visit of King George VI and his Queen to America in the summer of 1939, when the wives of two men of destiny looked into the overcast future unafraid. It was strengthened in those wartime days when Mrs. Roosevelt came over to front-line Britain to stay as a guest at Buckingham Palace, and endear herself to the King and Queen and their daughters.

The entourage at Clarence House is a comparatively small one. The Queen Mother took with her when she moved there her personal detective and the members of her own Household. Princess Margaret has her own lady-in-waiting, Miss Iris Peake, and her own maid, who has been with her—first in the capacity of under-nurse—since her childhood. Most of the Princess' secretarial work is done by Captain Dawnay, the Queen Mother's secretary. Her lady-in-waiting keeps her engagement book, which is becoming more and more crowded.

The absence of the Queen and the Duke of Edinburgh lays upon the younger sister of the Sovereign an added burden of public duties. Most girls of her age would be glad to shed it at the first opportunity, but not Princess Margaret. Probably she alone of all the members of the Royal Family—with the exception of the Queen Mother—really enjoys public life. While the Queen accepts it as her duty, her younger sister regards it as a pleasure. There is nothing of the popular conception of a Princess drearily sacrificing herself on the altar of Royal obligations about Princess Margaret. She enjoys every moment of her role. There is in her that touch of the theatrical, inherited from the Bowes-Lyons, which is completely absent in the Queen. The limelight has no terrors for her. She will face a crowd and deliberately grip and hold it with the sure technique of a veteran actress.

Yet in spite of this artistic strain, she understands the value of simplicity. She is passionately sincere in her emotions. Underlying her wit and superficial cynicism is a gentle, affectionate, and very sensitive personality. She is thoughtful, and, like all the members of the Royal Family, has in her character a strong religious bent. This was responsible for absurd rumors circulated at one time that she was preparing to enter a convent. The truth was that after her father's death, she turned for comfort to the Church which had held so prominent a place in his life. As it happened, her friend Miss Laura Smith had arranged to attend a series of Lenten Lectures given by the Bishop of Kensington, and the Princess accompanied her to every one.

There is complete understanding between the Queen Mother and Princess Margaret. Their two temperaments dovetail. The Princess has always been far more the daughter at home than the Queen, who was trained from her childhood in the independent role of Heir to the Throne, and who began her public life at sixteen. The position of the unmarried younger sister is no hardship to Princess Margaret, and she has been in no hurry to change it. All her friends know that she will never marry anyone she does not love. The devotion of her parents to one another set a high standard for her, which she will expect to fulfill in her own marriage.

In choosing a husband the first consideration with her will be whether he is the one man in the world for her. The second will be her family's attitude to the marriage. Legally she can marry anyone, provided the Queen gives her consent. But the Princess will want more than that. She will have to be assured that both her sister and her mother really approve of the match. She has never been the headstrong self-willed girl of popular imagination. Even as a teenager her challenge to parental discipline never extended further than the right to choose her own clothes. It was fun at eighteen to make her father frown by appearing in an off-the-shoulders evening dress—with the certainty that he could be coaxed afterward into an admission that it suited her. It would be quite another thing to embarrass a very loving sister, who in her position as Queen and Defender of the Faith is pledged to uphold the established religion of England, by imploring her consent to any marriage which would meet with the disapprobation of the Church. And Princess Margaret is far too aware of the responsibilities of her Royal rank to do this, however much she might wish it. As the daughter of a King she has had engrained in her from her earliest childhood the obligations of Royalty. That unspoken vow of loyalty toward the Monarchy, which is exacted from every member of a ruling house, will always be more important to her than any considerations of her own personal happiness.

This was the real answer to speculations as to the possibility of her marrying Group-Captain Peter Townsend, speculations which caused great distress both to the Princess and to the handsome young equerry who left his post in the Royal Household to take up an appointment as Air Attaché at the Embassy in Brussels. Those who quoted the case of the Duke of Windsor, and believed that his niece would follow his example, forgot one vital difference. The Duke of Windsor, at the time of his decision to marry Mrs. Simpson, was King Edward VIII, a ruling Sovereign, responsible to no other member of his family. Had his father been alive he would have been constrained by his duty as first subject in the land to give implicit obedience to the reigning monarch, and the story might have ended otherwise.

In the beginning color was given to the gossip regarding Group-Captain Townsend, which originated in the immediate Court circle, by the fact that he was so often seen in public with Princess Margaret. Exactly the same rumors of an impending engagement had been circulated in the past concerning the Princess' friendship with Lord Blandford and Lord Dalkeith, but in each case the stories had died for want of confirmation.

Group-Captain Townsend, on the other hand, because of his official position had a place in the Princess' daily life. She had known him since her childhood—when his sense of fun made him a favorite subject for practical jokes. King George VI, her dearly-loved father who had appointed him to the Royal Household, had been very much attached to him. The Queen Mother had leaned on him in the early days of her widowhood. He was a great friend of the Duke of Edinburgh. Naturally Princess Margaret saw a lot of him, especially at the time when the Queen Mother's Household moved into Clarence House, for he was entrusted with supervising the removal.

They had always had a great deal in common, shared the same tastes in music and in pictures, the same love of sports and racing. Both are passionately interested in flying, and when the Princess entered her own plane for the King's Cup Air Race, it was almost a foregone conclusion that she would choose Group-Captain Townsend to pilot it.

The final spark was probably applied to the train of rumor by the Amendment of the Regency Act, making the Duke of Edinburgh the first potential Regent. "To enable Princess Margaret to marry a commoner if she wishes," said the gossips, completely ignoring the fact that the Amendment was only following the precedent of Queen Victoria.

The Townsend speculations have died down, but others have arisen. Mr. Billy Wallace, one of London's most popular bachelors; Mr. Robin McEwen, son of a rich Catholic land-owning family; and Mr. Mark Bonham-Carter, one of the most intellectual young men in the Princess' set, and certainly the one whose conversation she most enjoys; have all been labelled by popular imagination as prospective husbands for her.

In the meantime she is unperturbed by the speculations. During the last few months she has acquired a new serenity. Her plans for the future, whatever they may be—and even her closest friends are afraid to prophesy—are obviously happy ones.

The Queen Mother, like her own mother, Lady Strathmore, has the wisdom not to attempt to dictate to her daughter. She is insistent on allowing her absolute freedom to live her own life. She believes that a parent's role is not to dominate but to help, and although she is looking forward to having Princess Margaret with her, and to entertaining for her, she is determined not to absorb her future. Those who know her best say that she not only realizes that Princess Margaret will probably marry one day, but that she would actually wish this. She herself made an ideally happy marriage, and she knows that her daughter's temperament is very akin to her own.

The afterglow of that marriage between the Duke of York and the Lady Elizabeth Bowes-Lyon is still reflected in the Queen Mother's quiet contentment today. The years have taken from her the bridegroom who stood beside her at the altar of Westminster Abbey on that spring morning of 1923, but nothing can efface the memory of their happiness. It is continued in the fullness of her life today; in the love her children have for her.

It is too early to foretell the place which history will one day give to this daughter of a Scottish laird who became a Queen of England. It will certainly remember the grace and dignity with which she fulfilled the great role so suddenly thrust upon her. It will remember her influence, as Duchess of York, on the home life of the nation in the cynical nineteen-twenties; her part in the general improvement of living conditions, and especially the care of children; her courageous example to the women of Britain in the war years.

But will it, I wonder, record of her the essential truth that here was a Queen who reigned not only by her husband's side over a nation, but supreme in her own home? Her influence, enshrined in the hearts of her children, will live far into the future.